Removing
Obstacles
to Success

Other books available by Dan Bobinski:

Creating Passion-Driven Teams

Hire, Train, & Retain Great Employees

Become a Student of Your Students
(with Jeralynne Bobinski)

The Teacher's Intellect:
Creating Conditions for Teaching & Learning
(with Dennis R. Rader)

Removing Obstacles to Success

Dan Bobinski

LEADERSHIP
DEVELOPMENT
PRESS

A Division of LEADERSHIP DEVELOPMENT, Inc.

ISBN-10: 0975943413
ISBN-13: 978-0-9759434-1-0

First Edition published August, 2015
Formerly published as *Living Toad Free* in 2003 with Dr. Dennis Rader

Published by Leadership Development Press
A division of Leadership Development, Inc.
10140 W. Meadowlark St., Ste. B, Boise, ID 83704

208-375-7606

Printed in the United States of America

Cover photo by Yanc, Used with permission
Cover design and book design by Leadership Development Press
Edited by Jeralynne Bobinski

In memory of

Dr. Dennis R. Rader

Killer of Toads

Inspiration

Friend

He is dearly missed

Removing Obstacles to Success

CONTENTS

Foreword

by William Glasser, M.D.

If you looked in the mirror and saw a Toad staring back at you, I'm sure you'd be alarmed. Instead of being alarmed, my advice is say to the image in the mirror, "Thank you very much for alerting me to the fact that I am unhappy." The Toad might then defiantly say, "That's my job—but now that you know you're unhappy, what are you going to do about it?"

Dan and Dennis have written a book that explains what you can do to move forward. Using Toads as a metaphor, they are asking you to consider dealing with all the important people in your life differently from the way you have for years—maybe since you were a very small child. Basically, this book is their way of showing you how to identify and give up the Toads in your life. Letting Toads rule over you is what I call external control psychology. Getting rid of Toads is what I call Choice Theory psychology.

Whenever you are unhappy you are relying on external control. External control harms our relationships and is by far the major cause of our unhappiness. Choice Theory teaches that we are social creatures, that the need for love and belonging is encoded into our genetic structure, and that good relationships are important to a successful life.

When you look back into your life you will see that whenever you were unhappy, you were relying on external control. *Living Toad Free* has plenty of examples of people using external control or Toady behavior that harmed their good relationships. But it also has good examples of people learning to replace their Toads with Choice Theory or happy, satisfying behaviors. Remember, you don't have to let the Toads hold you back—You can learn to choose a better way!

- William Glasser, M.D.
Author of *Choice Theory: A New Psychology of Personal Freedom* (1998) and *Warning: Psychiatry Can Be Hazardous to Your Mental Health* (2003).

Preface

As the late Dr. Dennis Rader and I put the finishing touches on the original book (then titled *Living Toad Free*) in 2003, we were spending a few days at a hotel in Northern Kentucky, away from our daily routines. It was early spring, and outside the windows of our hotel was a large green meadow framed against the backdrop of newly reborn green trees and beautiful rolling hills. Every morning, robins would descend on the meadow and spend their day looking for worms and eating bugs.

In reflecting on these birds, Dennis and I were reminded that God provides for all creatures. In the case of the robins, worms and bugs were provided daily, but the worms were not dropped in the robin's nests. Those birds had to get out there and look for their food!

In what might seem obvious to some, those birds were looking for food in a real meadow, not on Astroturf. They might have looked around on Astroturf at one point in time, but if they did, they soon realized it is futile to keep looking for nourishment in places where it does not exist!

By definition, the word "motivation" means "a reason to move." If God piped worms straight to the robin's nests, their bellies would be full but their hearts and wings would atrophy. Robins know they must move to get their food – their nourishment. They also know where they have to go to get it. Their reasons for movement are clear and consistent.

On the other hand, humans often move for reasons that are less clear and consistent. Sometimes we find ourselves looking for spiritual nourishment in what for us is the equivalent of Astroturf.

When that happens, we run the very real danger of becoming misdirected, and striving to become what we were never meant to be.

Parker Palmer, in his book *Let Your Life Speak: Listening for the Voice of Vocation*, was certain that he had been called to become a minister of the Gospel. But then things changed:

> So it came as a great shock, at the end of my first year [in seminary], God spoke to me—in the form of mediocre grades and massive misery—and informed me that under no conditions was I to become an ordained leader in His church.

Palmer went off to eventually find his true calling, as a teacher and a writer.

Whenever resistance fights against the force of your motivation (your 'reason to move'), you have to find out why. Is it something destructive inside yourself, or is it God's way of saying that the endeavor is not your vocation? Palmer writes:

> Vocation does not come from willingness. It comes from listening. I must listen to my life and try to understand what it is truly about—quite apart from what I would like it to be about—or my life will never represent anything real in the world, no matter how earnest my intentions.
>
> That insight is hidden in the word *vocation*, which is rooted in the Latin for "voice." Vocation does not mean a goal that I pursue. It means a calling that I hear. Before I can tell my life what I want to do with it, I must listen to my life telling me who I am.

We can safely assume that when we identify the kind of "food" that God designed for each of us as individuals, we won't find ourselves stymied by Toady conditions. In other words, the flow of our life gets easier when we align ourselves with our vocation.

The main focus of this book is those situations in which we encounter obstacles to motivation. While motivation is a reason to move, obstacles are what impedes that flow. It was decided to call these impediments Toads because it helps people to visualize them. (They are then also easier to identify and squash.) Toads prevent us from becoming who we should become; they are self-defeating beliefs and behaviors that we receive from others, or generate and nourish ourselves. In other words, Toads are obstacles to success.

Robins have no inner resistance to looking for food (their nourishment and fulfillment). If they are physically healthy, robins are out there every day hard at work. But when internal obstacles impede our flow in the pursuit of our vocations and motivations, we need to ask the question, "Why?"

Are we striving to do the wrong thing, something not connected to our true vocation? Or, are we harboring and nourishing Toads, unconsciously resisting our innate, God-created internal desire to move toward our potential?

It is my hope that this book will help more people find fulfillment in their vocations as well as eliminate the Toads that prevent them from answering the call to those vocations. There is much wisdom in learning to listen for the voice of your true calling, as well as learning how to ignore the ugly voices of Toads.

By the way, in another unique parallel, it is ironic that just as Palmer says we must listen for our calling, robins do not scratch and peck for worms and bugs; they "listen" and look carefully to find the nourishment they need. Bottom line, fulfillment begins with listening.

☙ ❧

I set before you life or death, blessing or curse.
Therefore, choose life. - *Deuteronomy 30:19*

A Few Clarifications

I would like to emphasize the difference between toads and Toads. The lower-case "t" toads in our gardens are just fine and they're great to have around. It's the upper-case "T" Toads in our heads that we want to eliminate.

So, just to call it to your attention and differentiate between the two, I'll use an upper-case "T" when talking about the Toads that hold us back—the Toads in our heads.

ALSO: It's important to remember that people are not Toads!

Please repeat that out loud: People are NOT Toads!

That said, people can act very Toad-like if they are 'infested' with a lot of Toads, but they themselves are *not* Toads.

One more thought: Removing obstacles to success (aka living Toad Free) is a lifelong process, so please be encouraged to keep learning about life skills. The more you learn, the more effective you will be in everything you do!

Section 1:
The Toad Concept

Uncultivated minds are not full of wild flowers, like uncultivated fields.
Villainous weeds grow in them, and they are the haunt of toads.
- Logan Pearsall Smith

Chapter 1

Why Toads?

A s you start reading this book, you might be scratching your head as to why Toads were selected as a metaphor for obstacles to personal and professional growth. Actually, several reasons exist. Some are more fun, and some are more factual. Let's start with a few of the more factual comparisons:

Toads: Toads haven't changed much over the ages. Toads have always been, well, *toads*.
Obstacles: All of us face obstacles in life. They're the same kinds of problems people have been having since the dawn of time. And, just like toads, the problems holding us back can be pretty ugly.

Toads: Toads can live almost anywhere. They start out as seemingly insignificant tadpoles. But once their metamorphosis is complete, tadpoles transform into full-sized toads.
Obstacles: Problems and obstacles exist everywhere. No matter where we live, seemingly insignificant events happen during our earliest years that bewilder us. From childhood on, we interpret these events and draw conclusions—about ourselves, others, situations, and life. These conclusions are not always accurate, and down the road these incorrect conclusions grow and prevent us from becoming all we are capable of being.

3

Toads: You may know of only a few types of toads, but dozens and dozens of toad varieties exist in the world in many different sizes, each with its own peculiar way of surviving.

Obstacles: The obstacles we face come in a wide variety of shapes and sizes. You may have awareness of a select group of personal issues that inhibit development. But many problems (both physical and mental) and self-defeating behaviors exist, and you may be unaware of them or know very little about them. The obstacles people face are many, each with its own way of persisting.

What I call Toads, other people may call "hang ups," "having issues," "personal problems," or "baggage." In more serious cases, psychologists may say a person has neurotic or self-defeating behavior. But I simply say someone has a *Toad*. It really doesn't matter what word people use, what we're talking about are obstacles to progress … things that stop us or slow us down.

Why Toads? Well, first of all, if we're going to be talking about changing our mindset and how we deal with obstacles, why not make it fun? Think about it: We rarely acknowledge that our internal fears are slowing us down. We humans are good at projecting blame onto others for our circumstances, or even blaming the circumstances themselves. And we do so because it's often too painful mentally and/or emotionally to acknowledge we have a fear holding us back.

Brave, close friends (or acquaintances that seem eager to fix us) may try pointing out the obstacles that are our fears, yet even when we can accept that frustrating pain, we still have a tough time "seeing" the fear. Fear is invisible. Internal obstacles are intangible. How do we deal with something inside our psyche that we can't see, and something that has no borders to wrap our hands around?

Enter the Toad.

Since most people are visual learners and since nebulous concepts do not make for user-friendly healing terminology, I say let's make it fun, and take whatever mental obstacle we have, and call it a Toad.

Psychologically, it gives us several huge advantages:

1. We are bigger than Toads. Staring down at a Toad, we have no doubt we could squash it if we needed to. There's no way we're getting taken down by a Toad.
2. It takes a nebulous concept (such as fear) and makes it tangible. Toads are defined. They have borders. We can manage something tangible more easily than something intangible.
3. Perhaps most importantly, we can picture the Toad being outside of us. It's difficult to deal with internal obstacles, because they seem interwoven into who we are. By transferring the "problem" to a small, insignificant Toad, we get it outside of ourselves, thus making it easier to manage.

Think about it. Anyone can easily visualize a Toad. If you doubt this, try this little test:

A psychologist says a client is suffering from agoraphobia.
I say the client has a big Toad sitting on the front step of his house, and the Toad won't let him go outside.

Assuming that you're not a seasoned psychologist, which is easier to picture mentally:
     a) agoraphobia, or
     b) the Toad?

If your answer is the Toad, this book is for you. (If your answer is agoraphobia, perhaps you should see—or be—a psychologist!)

Learning how to eliminate Toads, that is, removing the obstacles that lead to your success, begins with identifying the type of Toad in your way. The Toad may be huge, blocking the path that takes you to your goal, or small, jumping out to trip you up or distract you every time you walk down a particular path. By eliminating the Toads, usually accomplished by starving them or by going around them, you can continue on your way to live out your calling and your goals.

Bottom line, dealing with Toads takes an intangible problem and makes it tangible. Besides, why not take a normally uncomfortable process and work through it with a fun, easy-to-use metaphor?

In the first section of this book I'll talk about motivation and how internal obstacles prevent us from getting what we want. By the way, the Coach Hatfield story (chapter 2) does a good job of summarizing the Toad concept. Even children as young as 7 and 8 can grasp the metaphor, and you can use it for helping them get past what's holding them back.

In the middle sections I'll present a collection of "Toad stories," all of which are true (although the names and places have been changed to protect the innocent and shield the guilty). These middle sections have both Toad stories, and also Toad funerals. The funerals are stories that illustrate how people eliminated certain Toads that were hindering their lives.

In the last section of the book I'll present what I call "Tools for Toad Killers." More specifically, these will be things you can do to help eliminate Toads from your life.

As you read, have fun with the metaphor, and see if you can start identifying the Toads holding you back. After all, this book is about helping you remove the obstacles that are preventing you from achieving success, and from being all that God designed you to be.

I believe you can do it. You can eliminate the Toads in your life, and the concepts and tools in this book will help you do it. It is my strong belief that everyone has the right to remove the obstacles holding them back, and live Toad free!

You can outdistance that which is running after you,
but not what is running inside you.
- *Rwandan Proverb*

Chapter 2

The Coach Hatfield Story

C oach Hatfield knew about Toads. He knew where they came from, but more importantly he knew how to get rid of them. The key, according to Coach Hatfield, was to figure out what Toads were getting in the way, then eliminate them.

Coach Hatfield was a basketball coach at a small college in Illinois. He was tough, but he let everybody play. Most folks said he worked miracles, because somehow he developed winning teams in a school too small to really have the horses.

At the beginning of every season Coach Hatfield sat down with the new players and told them the following story:

"Mr. Centipede woke up early one morning in a great mood. He had a date later that day with the centipede of his dreams, Ms. Diana Centipede! She had one hundred of the longest legs he'd ever seen.

"Mr. Centipede showered, put on his favorite yellow socks and fifty pairs of black Adidas tennis shoes. He slicked back his hair, flashed himself a confident smile in the mirror and headed for the door. With every leg in perfect rhythm, he flowed out of his little cave on the side of the hill.

"As fate would have it, Mr. Centipede chanced upon Mr. Toad, sitting alongside the trail (on a toadstool, of course), in his usual toady frame of mind. Mr. Centipede, beaming confidence, stopped and raised ten of his legs in a friendly salute. 'Good Morning, Mr. Toad! How are you on this gorgeous day?'

"Mr. Toad gave Mr. Centipede an aggravated glance, then grumbled back, 'What's so good about it?'

"Realizing he didn't want to lose his good mood in debating with a toad, Mr. Centipede turned his head and answered to the air about the bright sun, the puffy clouds, and the fresh air. Then, starting up his jaunty, rippling body once again and with all his legs in perfect rhythm, he flowed past Mr. Toad.

"That's when it happened. Mr. Toad's brow furled as he watched Mr. Centipede glide past. Then a quizzical look came over the toad's scowling face as he called out to Mr. Centipede in a gruff, toady voice. 'Mr. Centipede! Stop! There's something I want to ask you.'

"Mr. Centipede stopped mid-stride, looked back over his shoulder, and said, 'What is it, Mr. Toad?'

"How do you do it, Mr. Centipede?"

"Do what?"

"Walk! How do you walk with all those legs in perfect unison? How in the world do you manage to move them all, much less at the same time?"

"Mr. Centipede tilted his head and thought about the question. And he thought. And then he thought some more. Mr. Centipede missed his date. In fact, Mr. Centipede never moved again!"

Then Coach Hatfield explained to his newcomers how Sammy Centipede had encountered a Toad of Confusion. "The Toad," Coach explained, "sent the centipede's state of mind into a whirlwind of doubt and confusion—totally taking him off guard. So much so that he froze."

The new ballplayers nodded as if they understood, but Coach Hatfield wasn't done yet. He showed them a plaque with an old sports saying engraved on it:

It's no sin to be blocked.
Only to stay blocked.

Then Coach Hatfield said, "There are a lot of Toads and Toady situations in life that trip us up. Fear Toads, Perfection Toads, Inferiority Toads, Superiority Toads, Intimidation Toads, Guilt Toads, you name 'em, they're out there! We've all got our share of them, and that's okay. What's *not* okay is to let any Toad, small or large, grow so big that it cripples us. The worst Toads, the biggest ones, are those that live in the confines of our own minds. Those are the Toads that we feed and care for ourselves—the ones we grow within our own thoughts."

The players were looking a bit confused, so Coach Hatfield threw the facts straight at them: "There are two kinds of basketball players. One is the guy fooling around on the playground. He isn't serious. Either he isn't committed or he hasn't got the guts or the brains to nurture his talent. The other kind has the courage and the fortitude to challenge the Toads preventing him from being the best he can be. Those without the dedication, the courage, or the perseverance to eliminate their Toads should go home now. You will become mature players in this game or you will be gone!

"Whenever a Toad knocks us down we're going to either get back up to knock it down or we're going to find a way around it! People who succeed at this game are just like people who succeed at life. They don't feed or pamper their Toads. Instead they find them and exterminate them! We will not allow any Toads to get in our way! Is that understood?"

It was understood. The Toad concept worked to bring the teams together every year. In fact, the shout of, "Kill the Toad! Kill the Toad!" became the team's rallying cry, much to the confusion of opposing teams.

Coach Hatfield used the Toad analogy all the time. He frequently chose his starters by looking each player in the eye and asking, "Are you Toad-free tonight?" And once, when the team's best player developed an attitude of superiority, Coach Hatfield helped him become the team's best "team-player" by showing him how his ego had become a Toad to the rest of the team.

Coach Hatfield's Toad stories taught his teams about resiliency and stamina. They learned to take the heavy blows and keep on

9

moving. Hence, they were never routed. Not only did they never quit as individuals, they "jelled" so well as a team they ended up winning games that, on paper, they weren't supposed to win. And whenever they were defeated, they were beaten by a genuinely superior team—never by themselves.

No matter what, his teams always kept their pride because they always maintained flow and momentum, maintaining integrity even in the face of overwhelming competition. Coach Hatfield called that character. No matter what the score or the reputation of the opposition, all of Coach Hatfield's players held onto their integrity. And they eliminated their Toads as soon as they recognized them.

‽ ∾

The Toad & the Centipede*

The centipede was happy quite
Until a toad, in fun
Said "Pray, which leg goes after which?"
This worked his mind to such a pitch
He lay distracted in a ditch
Considering how to run.

‽ ∾

*This is the poem from which Coach Hatfield created his Toad story. It is often titled *The Centipede's Dilemma*, and is usually attributed to Katherine Craster (1841-1874), due to it appearing in her 1871 book, *Pinafore Poems*.

Only when we are no longer afraid do we begin to live.
- Dorothy Thompson

Chapter 3

Fear is the Greatest Obstacle

Whenever I see something online about motivation or identifying obstacles to success, I often take time to read it. One day I came across a message board on Reddit.com called *Get Disciplined.* A post on that board caught my eye, and I immediately thought it would be good material for this book. Unfortunately, the person who made the post had deleted his/her username, so I can't give the person credit.

I thought the post made good, solid points that everyone should hear, but I also thought the person posting it had missed the fundamental truth that *fear* was at the root of all the obstacles mentioned. Then, as I continued reading the thread, I noticed someone with the username *aleatorictelevision* had posted a response that basically said what I wanted to say. And so, for your reading enjoyment, below are both posts.

The original post:

"In life there are four things holding you back from achieving greatness. Those four things are Fear, Doubt, Laziness, and Ignorance. Anything and everything that is holding you back from being awesome are these four things. Whether or not you know this, whether or not you realize this, every great

11

achiever has faced yet overcome these four things. In life these will come in different faces and in different forms but you must not only know, but master overcoming these. [In] any hobby, job, or passion you will be faced with these four things. So overcome them, because that is all that is holding you back.

The posted response that I liked:

Doubt is uncertainty of an outcome. Laziness is the lack of desire to achieve an outcome. Ignorance is the lack of knowledge to achieve an outcome. Ignorance leads to doubt. Doubt leads to laziness. Laziness leads to ignorance. A vicious cycle.

The cycle is based on fear. Fear of the outcome leads to doubt. Fear of the cycle and breaking the cycle leads to laziness. Fear of change leads to ignorance.

What fear? Fear of the future, of ourselves, [and] of the unknown fuels every nightmare and hinders every step. Fear is the mountain to be conquered, worse than any mortal enemy. Stare into its abyss and be eternally lost.

As I said, I like both posts, but the response underscores what I believe to be the truth: At the core of Doubt, Laziness, and Ignorance is Fear. Minimize the fear, and we weaken the other three obstacles. Remove fear, and the other three obstacles can all be removed more easily.

It is my position that almost every Toad that lurks in the corners of our minds is related to fear in some way. I urge you to remember that as you start weeding out the Toads trying to hold you back.

Myths operate in men's minds without them being aware of facts.
- *Claude Levi-Strauss*

Chapter 4

Exposing the Myth of Motivation

Perhaps you've accused someone of lacking motivation, or you've heard someone else use that phrase. Maybe you've even been accused of lacking motivation yourself. The problem? Believing that people lack motivation is bad psychology. The word *motivation* literally means "a reason to move," and everyone has a reason to move.

For example, you may think that a slow-moving co-worker lacks motivation, but when he zips out the door at the end of his work day, you *know* he has a reason for it. He has something he wants to go do. In other words, he's motivated!

Thus, if we want to help people who are "lacking in motivation," we'll need to expose that phrase for the myth that it is, and learn the truth about why people act (or don't act) on what they want or need to do.

Again, the word motivation means "a reason to move." When we're hungry, we find something to eat. When we're thirsty, we find something to drink. These are basic motivations. When we are hungry and thirsty, we are motivated (have a reason) to find food and drink.

The same can be said about desires. If we want to spend time vacationing at a plush resort, we are motivated (have a reason) to save

13

money for that vacation. If we want a promotion, we are motivated (have a reason) to go above and beyond our normal job responsibilities, learning and doing what is required for the new position.

However, over the years, I have found that what slows people down in life is not a lack of motivation, but rather the presence of obstacles. If motivation is a reason to move, obstacles are what get in the way of our movement. With that perspective, when someone isn't moving, it's usually not because he has no motivation. Instead, it's very likely that an obstacle is in his path. In truth, that obstacle is usually dwelling within the person's head. And, quite often, that obstacle is linked to some form of fear.

Let's consider this idea with the example of an outside sales rep who finds it hard to make cold calls. This man does not lack motivation to cold call—he knows he needs sales or he'll starve. Therefore, he certainly has motivation (a reason to move).

But if his sales manager adheres to the myth that he's not motivated, she may try different methods to increase his motivation. Maybe she'll offer him a bonus for achieving sales quotas, or a weekend trip for him and his family. These techniques may work, but if unseen obstacles exist, those solutions will work only in the short term, if at all.

To help understand this, let's use a word picture analogy. Let's equate motivation with a tire. This tire is the right size for our sales rep, and it moves him along in the direction he wants to go; In this case, making sales.

However, when our sales rep turns onto "Cold Call Lane," he encounters a rather large obstacle in the road (a fear of rejection), and his tire (his motivation) is just not big enough to go over the obstacle. Because he doesn't want to crash, he stops.

If his manager sees he's not moving but doesn't see the real size of the obstacle, she may send him to an exciting seminar where he learns to "pump up" his motivation so it's big enough to get over obstacles. He finds the seminar invigorating, and the next day he pumps up his tire so large that he rolls over the obstacle on Cold Call Lane with no problem. He spends the entire day on Cold Call Lane making lots of sales, and everyone is happy.

But, after a few days, the enthusiasm from the workshop is wearing off. By the end of the week all the extra air has leaked out of his tire and it is back to its normal size.

Unfortunately, the obstacle on Cold Call Lane is still there.

The next week our sales person tries pumping up the air in his tire, but the excitement from the seminar has dissipated. His tire can't seem to get big enough to move him over that pesky obstacle that remains in the road.

Frustrated, his boss tells him that he lacks motivation, and thinks about letting him go.

Many highly respected motivational speakers talk about the need to pump up our motivation. And, without a doubt, that technique works to get people over the obstacles in their way. However, what if we looked at getting past the obstacles in front of us with a different perspective? What if, instead of expending daily or weekly energy pumping up our motivation, we identified and removed the obstacles in front of us, or found a different path altogether?

Consider how much time and energy we spend pumping up our motivation over the course of a month or a year. If the obstacles were gone, then we would have no need to spend time and energy artificially inflating the size of our tires. Instead of spending time psyching ourselves up so we can get past the obstacles, we can have extra time for other things we want and need to be doing.

Granted, some external obstacles holding us back are permanently in place, but no law exists saying we must eliminate an obstacle, or that we have to go over it. Maybe we can go around it. Maybe we can go under it. Maybe another road can take us to our desired goal, and

15

what if that road has much smaller obstacles – obstacles that our natural motivation could easily overcome?

To summarize, it's a myth that we're not doing better because of lack of motivation. In reality, it's usually obstacles holding us back, and many of those are in our heads, existing in the form of fears. If we identify and minimize (or remove) the obstacles, we are much more likely to make progress on our goals.

Section 2:
Toads at Home

It seems to me probable that anyone who has had
a series of intolerable positions to put up with must have been
responsible for them to some extent.
- Robert Hugh Benson

Chapter 5

Mike and Margaret

Mike and Margaret were your typical, middle-class parents. Margaret, a little more ambitious and outgoing than her husband, had a real estate license and sold homes in their small suburban town. Mike, slightly built and more timid, worked as a certified mechanic at a local repair shop. He was quiet and found contentment working by himself and doing the job right.

With their two young children, Samantha and Paul, the family was as middle-of-the road as middle class gets. Margaret made sure that the children were involved in various activities, while Mike was glued to the TV on the weekends, sipping a beer or two, quietly watching whatever sport was in season. Margaret's mom, long divorced, lived just a few blocks away. Once or twice a month she'd come over and they'd all spend the weekend together.

One cloudy, cool morning, Mike was working at the shop as usual. He had his head under the hood of a car when he heard someone pull up just outside the service bay. Hearing a car door slam abruptly, Mike got out from under the hood to see a very angry person walking toward him. Non-confrontational by nature, Mike politely asked the man to step outside the service bay for insurance reasons. The man gave no hint of leaving. "What's up with this place?" the man yelled. "My wife comes here with a small knock in her engine and you guys milk her for $400?"

Mike looked out past the man at his car. It had been in the shop yesterday. "I recognize the car, sir, but I wasn't the one to work on it. Let me see if I can—"

Mike didn't have a chance to finish his sentence. The man was a ticking time bomb. "I don't care WHO worked on it, I want my money back!"

Mike shrugged and turned to go find the owner. The irate customer, thinking he was going to be ignored, let his fuse run out. He picked up a large pipe wrench and threw it at the back of Mike's head. Mike awoke to a couple of paramedics kneeling over him telling him that he was going to be all right.

As it turned out, the irate customer was arrested and Mike spent a day in the hospital for observation. After Mike was released, his boss gave him a few days off, but that didn't seem to be enough. The idea of getting his head bashed in for trying to provide good customer service didn't register. "What's it all for?" he thought.

A few days turned into a few weeks. Mike told his boss that he wasn't feeling up to coming back to work. The doctors had pronounced him fit, but Mike was uncomfortable about leaving the house. In fact, Mike was so withdrawn, he wouldn't even attend his attacker's court hearing.

After a month, his boss stopped by to talk. "I understand you might have some hesitancy about dealing with customers, but I need you at the shop, Mike, or we're going to have to let you go so I can hire somebody else."

Mike just stared at the wall. Silence permeated the room for what seemed like an hour. Finally Mike said, "That'd be okay."

Mike's boss paused. "I'm sorry to hear that," he said. After waiting a few more moments and looking at Mike with great concern in his eyes, he continued, "If you ever need to talk, just let me know." With that, Mike's boss got up and left, and Mike sat staring at the wall.

Margaret wanted to be there for her husband. She went to Mike the next day and told him that it didn't matter if he didn't work— she'd carry the financial load. In fact, she'd already crunched the numbers and, although it would be a squeeze, they could keep getting by on her income alone. Mike just nodded, and then said, "I'll keep up with the housework."

"Yes! That'll work!" Margaret said enthusiastically. It was an honorable way to explain the situation to their neighbors and relatives. "You can take care of the kids and the house, and I'll do the 9-to-5 thing! We're adaptable! We can do this!"

Margaret picked up the pace and showed more homes to compensate for the loss of Mike's income. Longer hours were okay in her mind, as long as she didn't let her family fall apart, as she perceived her mother had done so many years ago. Mike mostly sat around increasing his dosage of ESPN and any other sports he could find. He took comfort in his wife saying it was okay for him to stay home. By five o'clock he had done a few chores and dinner was on the stove. Once a week, he'd venture outside to mow the lawn and do some other yard work, but his days were mostly spent reading the newspaper and watching TV.

The children, Samantha and Paul, now in 3rd and 4th grades, were excited that Dad was going to be around when they got home from school. Now he could do things with them in the early afternoon, whereas before they were pretty much on their own. Sadly, their excitement waned as they discovered that Dad wasn't going to be too involved.

Inside their hearts the children were screaming for attention, but pulling Dad's eyes away from the TV was practically impossible. "I'm going to ride my bike, Daddy," Paul would often say, "Do you want to watch me?" "Sure," Mike said, without moving his eyes from the TV. Paul would run out to the garage, hop on his bike and ride it up and down the street. Each time he passed the house he would stick his hand up and wave, "Hi Daddy!" Sadly, Mike was oblivious.

After almost six months of this, Margaret stayed up late one night to talk with Mike. "Honey, I'm a little concerned," she said. "You're doing a great job of keeping up the house and all the work that needs to be done around here." She paused, and then said, "I'm just concerned that we're a little disconnected. The kids haven't said anything, but I can see that they don't feel you care."

Mike got defensive. "Don't care? Of course I care! I do their laundry, I vacuum their floors, I fix their dinner, I take care of them just fine! If that's not caring, I don't know what is!" He bristled at the thought that somehow he was inadequate.

Margaret wasn't prepared for Mike's defensive posture and loud tone of voice. Not wanting to upset the picture of a peaceful home, she backed down quickly, and just quietly asked Mike to engage more with the children. "Yeah, yeah, of course," Mike replied, but both of them knew nothing was going to change.

Margaret's mother began spending extra time with the children. She tried to support Margaret as best she could. Mike, however, continued to exclude himself from the rest of the world—except for his newspaper and sports television.

Over the years, Margaret got the children involved in soccer and little league. Asking Mike to attend any of their games always resulted in a, "No." The children knew better, but Margaret would always ask a second time. "Come on, Mike, don't you want to see the kids play?" "I don't feel like going," was Mike's regular reply, and his voice tone always indicated that it was final.

Once Margaret even suggested that she and Mike go in for some marital counseling. "Not on your life," Mike replied. "We're doing just fine. The bills are getting paid, the house is kept up, and nothing needs fixing—in the house or in the marriage."

The world went by, and Mike continued on his path of self-defined peaceful existence, unencumbered by the troubles of work or family issues. The children went on to graduate high school, but Mike found a reason for not attending either ceremony.

Eventually the nest was empty and Margaret and Mike were at home alone. Margaret saved her money and started taking little vacations every few months, alone. She always stayed faithful, as she didn't want her marriage—what little there was of it—to break up like her mom's did. But after the kids were gone, Margaret was one of the loneliest people on the face of the planet.

Thoughts on Mike and Margaret:

As is usually the case, more than one Toad exists in this story. When Mike was assaulted, a Toad jumped on him and told him to stay away from people. That Toad then invited other Toads to join in the fun of freezing Mike's potential, by separating him from his life. Mike did nothing to stop this. Perhaps in Mike's youth he was never told he could shake off the Toads. Perhaps a Toad jumped on him and said that he needed these Toads to be safe. Often times, Toads compel us to dig ourselves into holes and then convince us of their comfort.

Whatever the reason, Mike chose to keep Toads around and feed them. They got comfortable, convincing Mike that he should continue to feed them – for if they were comfortable, Mike would never again have to experience the possibilities of risk, fear, or loss. Unfortunately, Mike believed their lies. He believed his marriage was just fine. Intentional ignorance guaranteed his sense of safety.

Margaret couldn't bear the thought of letting her family fall apart. Her parent's breakup so many years before had given birth to a Toad that told her she shouldn't let anything come between her and her husband. Her determination led her to neglect healthy boundaries and responsibilities in the family, but at what expense? The opposite of development is diminishment. She could say that she didn't let her family fall apart, but, in reality, that is exactly what happened.

If we are parents, we have the responsibility to be good parents. If we are workers, we have the responsibility to be good workers. If we are spouses, we have the responsibility to be good spouses.

In the end, we can be sympathetic to the plight of Mike and Margaret, but perhaps even more sympathetic for their children. There is no doubt that through all of this, they acquired some Toads that will impact them negatively at some point in their lives.

Men can starve from a lack of self-realization
as much as they can from a lack of bread.
- *Richard Wright*

Chapter 6

Twin Toads of Different Mothers

Helen's story:

In the upper-middle class circles of my Massachusetts upbringing, my parents made it clear that family reputation came first. My mother and father devoted their time to the club and other social events. It sometimes felt like my needs took a back seat, but they were doing the right thing.

Yet, despite the talk and appearance of family love, arguments and criticism were common at home. Father said good arguing kept us mentally sharp, but it was to be contained within the family. It made sense to me, so I never told anybody else about it.

Mother was critical of everything I did, but said she did so to help me become a strong woman. I eagerly desired her approval so I went along with it. Even if we just had an argument and then went outside and ran into a neighbor, everything would have to be sugary sweet among us. After all, we were a "loving stable family." Neighbors had no need to know of our personal matters.

I went to an Ivy League college, earned a master's degree, and then got a prestigious position at a Fortune 500 company. The business social scene became the centerpiece of everything I did. I dedicated myself to my work and my involvement with several service organizations.

Unfortunately, it seemed I would never marry. I dated on and off, but somehow seemed to intimidate all the men I met. Before I knew it I was 34 and still single.

Finally I met Craig. He had only an associate's degree and had bounced around in different career fields, which bothered me, but I liked him. Mom said that Craig was probably an irresponsible, playboy bachelor. "After all," she once told me, "he's 29 and doesn't have a stable career!" Even though my parents were against the marriage, I thought Craig needed someone like me in his life. Looking back, though, I wish I had known how difficult he was going to be. I never would have married him.

Craig's story:

I met Helen at a symphony concert. She showed an interest in me, and since I was new in town, I took an interest in her interest.

I'd recently landed a job as a department manager at a large retail store and was trying to improve my life. Helen seemed to come from a good upbringing. "Maybe," I thought, "if I marry someone like Helen I can get away from 'the wrath of Mom.'"

Ah, yes—Mom. Always sticking her nose in my business, telling me what to do. I wish my dad had taught me a few things about being a man, but he always deferred to mom. And all she ever said was, "Don't make waves." I wish I had a dime for every time mom told me, "you should" or, "you ought to…" Then there's the ever popular, "because I said so," even into my adult years.

I bolted right after high school to get away from the family, taking a bus to Washington D.C. where I got a job in construction. I learned a few skills and made a few friends, but construction life was not my cup of tea. I got out after one season and dinked around taking classes at a junior college in Virginia.

I wasn't sure what I wanted to do for a career, but my mom's nagging me to get a job "no matter what" put pressure on me. Her oft-repeated sentence rang through my head on a regular basis: "Get a job, get married, and everything will be okay." That was her formula—not that it worked for her and dad.

When I met Helen, I liked that she was friendly, outgoing, and comfortable meeting people. Considering I preferred to sit in the shadows, I figured I could learn a lot from her. She had a few quirks, but I thought I could overlook her peculiarities.

Then, two weeks before the wedding, I got into a huge argument with Helen's mother. She wanted me to get a better college degree and get more involved in socially relevant activities. She didn't seem to realize she was insulting me and implying I was incompetent.

It shocked me when Helen sided with her mother. I couldn't believe my ears! I wanted to call off the wedding, but the invitations had already been sent out. After much angst, I decided I shouldn't make waves and upset my family who had already bought airline tickets. So the wedding remained on the books. Besides, in the back of my mind I thought maybe Helen's mom was right.

Two weeks *after* the wedding, I realized I should have made waves. My life became a virtual hell of verbal and emotional abuse. I shouldn't have cared about the lousy few hundred bucks for people's airfare. You just can't put a price on sanity.

After three years of living hell, I couldn't take it anymore. Helen and I divorced. I just couldn't take all her cutting remarks about how inept and wrong I was every time I disagreed with her. If I said black, she said white. If I said white, she said black. Even after seeing numerous counselors, she wouldn't let up. I had to leave before I killed myself.

Jerry's story:

Craig was a buddy I met while working construction. He was alright, but also the kind of guy who was always telling me how I "ought" to be doing something when he wasn't so sure himself. We both got out of the construction business about the same time, and then wound up taking some classes together.

When Craig told me about Helen, I kept a "wait and see" approach. I knew Craig had been through a few women before. I'd watched him screw up relationships with women who would have been wonderful partners for him. I thought he had a few things to learn about giving and receiving love. Besides, Helen was from upper class society, and Craig was not.

My wait and see approach was wise: Helen turned me off the moment I met her. She was very controlling and treated me like I shouldn't do anything without her approval. "Wow," I thought. "This is going to be the match made in Hades." Unfortunately, every time I expressed my concern to Craig, he brushed me off.

Against my better judgment, but out of friendship with Craig, I was best man at their wedding. The ceremony and reception seemed to set the tone for their entire marriage. Craig was tense, and Helen kept telling him to lighten up. And their mothers both wanted to be in control. The tension created by both of their mothers was so thick you could cut it with a knife.

Their marriage lasted three years, but my involvement with them stopped after just six months. From the start, I couldn't stand Helen's constant opinion about what I should or shouldn't be doing. And although Craig spoke ill of his home life when the two of us would get together, he kept indicating I shouldn't make waves whenever we were with his wife. It was crazy. I can't see how anything is worth playing all those games.

Thoughts on Helen and Craig:

Both Helen's and Craig's upbringings taught them to adopt their mothers' Toads. Helen's mom had a "Portray a Loving Family" Toad, while Craig's mom had a "Don't Make Waves" Toad. Plus, both mothers planted and nurtured an "Approval Dependency" Toad in each child. In the end, the dynamics between Helen and Craig guaranteed a sham of a marriage.

Removing obstacles includes the idea that if you want something to happen, you find a way to make it so. Facing fears is a big part of that. If Helen and Craig had found the courage to face the Toads that were sucking the life out of their marriage, then perhaps their love would have had a chance. Intentional ignorance or cowardly inaction, while common, are never good responses. A better approach is to first acknowledge that fears exist. Then the specific Toads must be clearly identified before they can be eliminated.

All truths are easy to understand once they are discovered;
the point is to discover them.
- Galileo Galilei

Chapter 7

Why Wrap Hamburgers in Paper?

(A Toad Funeral)

Toad Funeral Notice: Remember that this book has two types of stories: Those in which Toads are still at work and those in which Toads have been eliminated. For the stories in which Toads are still at work I include a postscript section, analyzing the situation and considering alternatives for the people in the stories. Toad Funerals are the stories in which Toads have been eliminated (or are on the way out). For the most part, the funeral stories are clear about how a Toad was eliminated or avoided, so I usually let the story speaks for itself. However, occasionally I include an "Editor's Note" at the end, as I do in this following story.

B ob's story:

As a sales rep, I travel more than I'd like to. My wife and kids are on their own several times a month while I'm away, but the job pays well so I stay with it. Recently, I managed to schedule two presentations in Pittsburgh on the same day—one in the morning and one in the afternoon. That way I could fly up early in the morning and get back in a one-day trip.

On the morning of the flight, I found myself wishing it were an overnighter. I needed a day or two away. My eight-year-old son had been a handful lately and I was exasperated with him.

It was a relief to leave the house that morning. I flew in to Pittsburgh early and my first meeting was finished by 11:00 a.m. As I was putting things away, I realized I'd forgotten some papers back at the office and needed to stop at a copy shop before my afternoon appointment, so I politely declined a lunch invitation. By noon, I had what I needed and decided to stop by Burger King to grab a quick burger while preparing for my afternoon presentation.

Two minutes after sitting down to eat lunch and review my notes, I heard a little girl's voice. "Why do we use these trays?" Although she was not yelling, her lungs were obviously strong and her voice carried well. I must have been sitting 30 feet from the register area and she was loud and clear. I looked up to get a glimpse of this vociferous little girl and then returned to my work.

Less than a minute later, I heard her again, loud and clear: "Why do they wrap the hamburgers in paper?" My thoughts drifted away from my work, and I couldn't help remembering fielding questions like that from my own kids when they were her age. "Whew! I'm glad I don't have to do that anymore," I mused.

Then, the fact that I had to go back home that night and deal with my eight-year-old gave me an unsettled feeling. I pushed the thought away and felt a little sorry for the girl's father, who was escorting her through the crowded dining area. I felt a sharp twinge of aggravation when this little brunette with the powerful lungs and her father sat down at the table next to me. "Why do we use straws?" she asked, as she pushed her straw through the slots in the soda cap.

I fought giving a scowl to this little girl with the insistent voice, struggling inside to think through my afternoon presentation. Question after loud question popped out of this girl's mouth, seemingly one every five seconds: "Why do they put lettuce on hamburgers? Why do they put pickles on hamburgers? Why is bread brown? Why is ketchup red?" My focus was blown out of the water.

The questions went on and on, incessant, non-stop, and everlasting. Not only could I not focus on my notes, I couldn't even

30

think my own thoughts. In a matter of minutes, I was fixated on what question this girl would ask next. The questions kept coming and coming.

Frustrated, I thought about getting up and moving to my car where I knew I could have some peace and quiet. As I sat contemplating how to regain my sanity, I suddenly heard something else besides the girl's questions: I heard her father's responses. It was like something switched in my brain. I sat up a little straighter and paid closer attention.

After each loud question, the father responded in a quiet and respectful way, giving a concise answer in a loving tone. Never did his voice sound exasperated or condescending, only loving and accepting.

At this point, her sheer inquisitiveness and his loving, respectful responses pushed the Toad of Intolerance out of my head. My mind shifted from being distracted to being intrigued. This was a wonderful example of good parenting.

Whether or not the father knew it, his respectful responses were nurturing in this little girl a natural curiosity. I pictured her twenty years from now, having unwavering confidence that her questions were valuable and important, and that she would get answers.

This little girl was not going to go through life feeling repressed or diminished. Her approach to life would be one of empowerment and inquisitiveness; a life where she feels like she's worth something and her initiative matters.

I closed my notes for my afternoon meeting and smiled. I made a mental note to pay more attention to my own son's questions, and to respond in a loving, respectful tone. That would start as soon as I got home, and suddenly I was glad I was flying back that evening. I wrapped up the rest of my hamburger to go and broke out my phone so I could call home.

Editor's Note:

We often carry around Toads that raise their ugly heads when we think our "space" has been invaded. Although privacy is a good thing (and a healthy thing), we grow the most when we reach out and look at other's perspectives. It is too easy for us to get caught up in our own worries while neglecting the needs of those around us.

The little girl in this story was learning about initiative: how to be confident and creative in exploring the world. And her father was doing a great job of creating a Toad-Free environment for her.

The story teller was sensitive enough to see past his own Toads and, as a result, experience growth as a parent and a person.

If you are distressed by anything external, the pain
is not due to the thing itself, but to your own estimate of it;
and this you have the power to revoke at any moment.
- Marcus Aurelius

Chapter 8

My Toughest Toad

(A Toad Funeral)

Larry's story:

I wasn't born with a golden spoon in my mouth, but I have had a good life. Everything has gone as planned with relatively few deviations. I grew up in a large family, poor as worldly things go but rich in experiences with family and friends. In particular, I enjoyed working with my Dad. My parents divorced when I was small but my Dad was always there even though I didn't live with him. He had his own business and I grew up working alongside him. If I needed help emotionally, spiritually or financially, he was always there to smooth the path.

I married the perfect girl, started a family, and began a successful career. Dad went through some rough times, going through a divorce from his second wife, retirement, and eventually an illness that slowed him way down. Still, for me, things seemed fine, and I thought it was great when Dad moved next to me so that I, along with my family, could take care of him.

Eventually, Dad became even more ill. He had a mild stroke, became addicted to some of the medications that were supposed to help him, and had periods of total hallucinations where reality left

33

him. Even at this point, I was optimistic that he would get better. We consulted with other doctors and finally got him on some different medications. Dad was strong. He had overcome a lifetime of obstacles. Surely he could overcome this.

December 8, 1998. My brother, his family, and my wife's parents were at my house for Sunday dinner and to celebrate my 8-year old daughter's baptism. Dad was too sick to attend, so we sent a plate of food over with my 12-year old son so Dad could at least enjoy the food.

Enter the Toad.

My son soon came running back. His grandfather was on the floor with his head bleeding.

Slow motion. Blurred vision. We all ran the 75 yards to his mobile home. I got there first. Saw him…saw the blood…saw the .22 rifle that he had taught me to hunt with 30 years before.

It would be a gross understatement to say my life changed at that moment. Everything that ever made sense to me was gone. To attempt to make any sense out of the whole situation was fruitless. I can only describe the effects of this Toad as falling into the deepest, darkest pit one can imagine. I was swimming in mud, unable to breathe. Months and months of reliving, re-enacting, re-writing the script. It never changed though. The ending always came out the same, no matter how much I tried to change it.

I've always been a Toad killer. I welcome challenges, obstacles, and mountains to climb. I tell my wife that I'm more comfortable when we are struggling with money or some other hardship because it makes me work harder. When things are too easy I get antsy.

This Toad, however, was different, because it wouldn't die. I came at it from all angles. I sought God, blamed God, and hated God. I sought counseling. I turned more inward than I ever had before. I closed off my own wife and children for months, even though I knew that was the worst thing to do. I didn't care.

The name of this Toad, of course, was Guilt. There was no doubt in my mind that it was my fault that my Dad ended his own life. I was, after all, his caregiver. I had fed him, medicated him, and even

34

dressed him at times. I was "responsible." How could I be so careless as to allow this to happen?

Now, years later, things are better, but this story is not over. The Guilt Toad still appears from time to time. I wrestle with him now and then, but that's an improvement because we wrestled non-stop for about a year. Now it's only every month or two that he pops his head up, and the wrestling sessions are getting shorter and shorter. And even though it's always a struggle, I always win.

I may never kill this Toad, but one thing is for sure: This is my toughest Toad. All other Toads I meet along the road pale in comparison. I can kill them in a millisecond.

As a result of facing the Guilt Toad, I've become stronger, and more resolute. I stopped blaming God. I seek Him once again, because I realize it is He who brought me full circle back to normality. I've also reconnected with my family, gaining a new appreciation of their importance to me.

It has been a long road, and I don't want to travel it again. I realize that this Toad could have destroyed me had I let it. But now I have hope back, I have God back, and I have my family back.

Section 3:
Toads at School

The authority of those who teach
is often an obstacle to those who want to learn.
- *Cicero*

Chapter 9

The Suppression of Lisa

D r. Morris first met Lisa when visiting one of his student teachers at an elementary school in Florida. When he entered the first grade classroom, he noted the student teacher engaged with a small group of kids in a reading exercise. The regular teacher was giving a math lesson to another, larger group. A few children were busy at their individual desks. One of these got up and came over to him.

"Hello, my name is Lisa. You must be Dr. Morris. I understand that Miss Haynes is your student. As you can see, she is very busy, but I can help you."

"Why, thank you," Dr. Morris replied, impressed with the initiative and articulateness of this little girl.

"This is the most comfortable chair in the room. From here you can observe everyone. We all love Miss Haynes, by the way." Lisa turned to leave, but politely offered, "If there is anything else that I can do for you, just let me know."

Dr. Morris expressed his appreciation and Lisa went back over to her desk to continue working. He observed his student teacher, who was doing fine. He had no doubts about her to begin with, and it was readily apparent that she and the children worked well together. All the children were engrossed in the lesson.

Five minutes went by, then Lisa got back up from her desk and came over to him. "Perhaps you would like to talk with some of the other students? I could arrange that for you."

This initiative so intrigued Dr. Morris that he agreed that it would be a good idea. Lisa went to several of the sitting students and spoke quietly with them. One at a time, politely and quietly, each student came over to Dr. Morris to answer any questions he might have.

At the end of the school day, Dr. Morris could not wait to ask the teacher and his student about this precocious young leader who had such poise and ability when only in the first grade.

"She was like this from the very first day," informed the teacher. "She knew how to read and get along with everybody. She stayed after class to offer me her services. She said she could take over one of the reading groups if that would be helpful. I didn't have the slightest doubt that she could handle it, so I gave it a try in a limited sort of way, and it has worked out. I was afraid that the other kids would find her bossy but she somehow avoids that altogether. They like her and listen to her."

Dr. Morris always looked forward to visiting the class with Lisa. He felt that she was a natural born leader. He wondered what amazing things lay ahead of her.

Everything went well for that year, but as summer approached, Lisa's teacher became concerned. She asked Dr. Morris if he had any advice for the approaching predicament. "Both of the second grade teachers run a tight ship. I have talked with them but they both say that Lisa is a student and should be treated like one. I think they will feel a little threatened by this amazing little girl. They will fear that she is trying to take over the class to undermine them in some way."

The teacher continued, "I tried to tell them that this is not where Lisa is coming from. She just wants to be helpful and has a natural ability to organize the other kids and get things done. But they don't want to hear it. That's not the way they see students."

Dr. Morris did not know what to advise regarding this predicament. He felt Lisa's teacher had done all she could do. Students like Lisa did not fit into standard approaches to schooling, and they were threatening to teachers who focused on classroom management.

When school started up in the fall, Dr. Morris didn't have a student teacher in Lisa's second grade class, but he took the time to visit her once and checked through the window in the door a few times. Lisa was still friendly and confident, but she looked a bit anxious.

In the third year, Dr. Morris did not have a student teacher in Lisa's school. Nonetheless, he stopped by to visit her once. She seemed subdued, so much so that he asked the assistant principal about her. The assistant principle was concerned, as Lisa had not gotten along well with either her second or third-grade teachers. Nothing specific—just a general attitude of resistance and resentment.

Dr. Morris often thought about Lisa. He kept in contact with her first grade teacher, who also worried about the little girl. Both he and she hoped Lisa would have better luck with her fourth grade teacher, but it was not to be. He was not able to visit Lisa's school until half-way through the school year. When he went to the office to ask about Lisa, he was informed that Lisa was no longer at the school. She had been withdrawn by her parents and was now being homeschooled.

Dr. Morris met with Miss Haynes and they decided to visit Lisa at home. They set up an appointment.

Lisa's mother was friendly and cordial. She invited them into the house and offered them coffee. They could feel the tension and sadness in the home. At one point, in response to their concerns, Lisa's mother broke into tears.

"I don't know what happened to my little girl. She started school so far ahead. She could read and do math. She was confident and always so eager to help. Now she will barely come out of her room, even to meet with people I know she likes. The doctors keep trying to tell me that she's agoraphobic, but how could that be? What happened to my little girl?"

Thoughts on the Suppression of Lisa:

Frankly, this story infuriates me and makes me cry all at the same time. The Toads in this story are the education system itself and the Toads that live in the heads of teachers who prioritize classroom management over student development. It's also why I'm a strong proponent of homeschooling children from the start, so children aren't crushed by "the system" and can grow and develop into all that God intended for them.

Lisa's confidence and leadership capabilities do not align with the images in the heads of many teachers regarding how teaching and learning are supposed to occur. To those people, students are supposed to sit passively at their desks, listen attentively, and take notes or follow instructions. Teachers are to stand in front of classes and talk. For these Toads to be removed, much work lies ahead, but changes are not likely to happen in our lifetime.

My strong recommendation is this: Whenever possible and however possible, homeschool your children if at all possible.

One More Thought:

Consider this: It's been forty years since Lisa's parents removed her from that stifling environment. The world is in crisis, and needs a phenomenal leader. But Lisa is not available. Her potential was crushed at school.

By the way, do remember that all of these are *true* stories. This *really happened*. Only the names and places have been changed.

Nothing is rarer than a solitary lie; for lies breed like toads;
you cannot tell one but out it comes
with a hundred young ones on its back.
- *Washington Allston*

Chapter 10

The Case of the Missing Watch

It was an ordinary day in a small town classroom in East Tennessee. During morning break on the playground, Mrs. Roberts wore a varied collection of bracelets and watches on her wrist as she stood watching the children. She served as the safe repository of these items as her students zoomed about. She had been doing this for years and never gave it a second thought, but that was all about to change.

At the end of recess, the children lined up to retrieve their bracelets and watches. Billy was in the line, and asked in a puzzled voice, "Mrs. Roberts, where is my watch?" She looked down to see that her wrists were empty except for her own watch. Then she remembered that Billy had not given her his watch, and she told him so. Billy looked confused, said, "Oh," and turned away.

At that point, Renee, another student, stepped forward and said, "Billy did give you his watch, Mrs. Roberts, I saw him do it." With this announcement Billy turned about from his confusion, as he too, became certain that he had given Mrs. Roberts his watch. Puzzled, Mrs. Roberts directed her students back to the classroom, then took Billy down to the office to report his missing watch.

When she got back, the entire class was distracted. Mrs. Roberts knew why, but she didn't know what to do about it.

During lunch, she overheard one of her students telling another, "Mrs. Roberts took Billy's watch." By the time lunch was over, the predicament had grown into a full-blown Toad. No more learning was going to happen that day, and if the situation wasn't resolved, the problem was going to become permanent.

Mrs. Roberts was curious about Renee. The little girl was normally shy, yet she had stepped forward and intentionally lied about Billy handing over his watch. Why?

She took Renee and Billy aside and asked them both once again if they were certain. Renee repeated her assertion without hesitation, and Billy followed suit. He was certain, also.

Mrs. Roberts needed a solution, and she needed it now. She took her class back to the playground and had them sit in a circle. She then chose a couple of students she trusted absolutely and spread them out to search the playground for the watch. She asked Billy to retrace his steps. He told her that he had become involved in a ball game. "And what were you doing before that?" she asked, "I was carrying a book from the library," Billy replied. "And where did you put the book while you were playing?" she asked. "Over here by this bush," Billy said, as he walked in that direction.

There, by the bush, was the watch.

Billy immediately apologized to Mrs. Roberts and then told the class about his mistake. But Renee did not apologize. Even when confronted with proof of her lie, she glared back at Mrs. Roberts with a frozen, stubborn stare. The predicament was not over.

Thoughts on the Case of the Missing Watch:

Never assume that Toads will disappear on their own if they are ignored. That approach often allows Toads to find a comfort zone and begin claiming territory. Mrs. Roberts was right to call a search for the watch to halt further Toad growth.

In children, the sudden appearance of a Toad is often caused by something happening in the home. Mrs. Roberts should tactfully express concern to Renee's parents. Situations such as these always call for the highest level of professionalism in a teacher.

Follow your instincts --
and don't let other people's opinion of you
become your opinion of yourself.
- Sarah Jessica Parker

Chapter 11

Santa's Doll

(A Toad Funeral)

R osie's story:

I grew up in east Texas in an area they call The Big Thicket. We were poor, but I didn't think about it much until I started school. All my clothes were hand-me-downs from my older sister. They were already stained, torn, and threadbare, and everybody knew my situation. Kids notice that kind of thing, and they were not kind.

Then, when I was ten, my father was killed in a car accident, hit by a drunk driver on his way home from work in the fields. There was, of course, no insurance, and the drunk had no money. He spent a few months in jail and then disappeared. At the time of my father's death, my mother was five months pregnant with my sixth sibling. That made seven kids without a father. Somehow, Mom managed to support all of us and to this day I don't know how she made it.

I remember when I was in the fifth grade, we were getting ready for the school Christmas program. It was a big deal and everyone was excited. The teachers from both classes in our little school wrote on the chalkboard what roles would be available and told us to think about which ones we wanted to be.

I knew instantly that I wanted to be one of the dolls. I told my best friend and she agreed that I would make a pretty doll.

45

That afternoon, during recess, I was playing outside when three snobby girls from my class came up to me. These girls were really popular, especially with the boys. They wore the nicest clothes and were mean and rude to those of us who did not. The only time they spoke to me was to tease and make fun of me. They told me I could not be one of the dolls because only three were needed and they were going to be them. And they always got their way.

"Besides," one of them said, "Santa does not make brown dolls and you never wear pretty dresses anyway."

Then one of the other girls said, "Why don't you be one of the reindeer? They are brown like you."

I felt so bad that I wanted to cry, but I didn't. I was not about to give them the satisfaction of hurting my feelings once again.

I went home that night feeling sorry for myself and started crying. The more I thought about it the more I decided they were right. I was a poor Mexican girl with no pretty dress to wear and I had no right to have a major role in our Christmas Program—a program my mother wouldn't even be able to attend because she worked the night shift at the factory where they made frozen dinners.

The next day at school, our teacher asked us what we wanted to be. I had decided the night before that I was going to be either an elf or a reindeer. When she got to me, I just about said "elf" but instead I blurted out, "DOLL!"

All heads turned and looked at me because word on the playground was the doll roles were already spoken for, but in that split second my mind was made up. I was going to be a doll no matter what.

I thought, "I may be brown and poor, but somehow or another I could still be one of Santa's dolls." I wasn't going to allow other peoples' opinions of me get in the way of my wants and needs.

Well, I got the part! And my mother ended up buying me a dress that was yellow with white ruffles from the department store in town. She worked overtime just so she could do it.

I remember feeling so special the night of the Christmas program. My dress was the prettiest one of all; prettier than any of the ones that the snobby girls wore. Even one of the teachers told me so. My mother wasn't able to attend because of her work, but my sister and all my brothers attended, and we told my mother all about it.

In many ways, I feel like my whole life has been a lot like the area where I grew up…pretty much a Big Thicket…lots of thorny obstacles that are tough to get around. But the day that I stood up for myself and told the world what I really wanted to be gave me the courage to keep on doing it. All things considered, since that time, I've done pretty well.

I sometimes wonder what would have become of me if I had settled for being an elf or reindeer.

Editor's Note:

This is yet another true story illustrating the pain kids must deal with when in institutionalized schooling. Hats off to Rosie, who took a stand and refused to be bullied. What comes to mind is a statement once made by Eleanor Roosevelt:

> A snub is the effort of a person who feels superior to make someone else feel inferior. To do so, he has to find someone who can be made to feel inferior.

Something came alive in Rosie the moment she said, "DOLL!" She wasn't going to be made to feel inferior, and it changed her life forever.

> It's alright to have butterflies in your stomach.
> Just get them to fly in formation.
> *- Dr. Rob Gilbert*

Chapter 12

Running Through the Toads

(A Toad Funeral)

Ann's story:

Three or four times a week, I put on my Toad-killing armor. I change into shorts, sports bra, tank top, and running shoes. Until recently, I had no idea that this was amphibian-eliminating attire. Now when I run, instead of thump-thump-thump, I hear squish-squish-squish. The track is littered with Toad carcasses; so many that they are hard to avoid. There are the usual Toads: Malaise, Homework, and Just-don't-feel-like-it. They are easier to ignore every day, because the more I go on the Toad-killing sprees, the more miracles happen, the more evidence is amassed proving that I am not wasting my time in college.

The next set of usual Toads hop up once I start running harder: Side-ache, Muscle-ache, Breathlessness, and Nausea. Nausea is particularly fond of me lately. Oh, and the little one that almost looks innocent: That little Toad that says, "It's OK to quit, you've had a rough day."

Some days these guys are easier to beat than others. Some days they win, but those days are rare and I am winning the war as long as I come back for another battle.

After I've been running a few laps, other Toads appear. Usually they are things I've felt bad about the last couple days. Often it's Self-Doubt, or that not-so-little voice that says, "You're not good enough, not smart enough, or not well liked." These are the Toads wandering around in my mind, often occupying my thoughts in between counting laps. But as each leg moves me down the track, I almost invariably kill, mutilate, and disintegrate the remains of the Toads that have, until recently, held me back.

Physiologically, I can explain why I enjoy running: Exercise is proven to increase endorphins, which elevate mood and combat depression. But there has to be more. Perhaps it's just spending the time untangling the knots in my mind.

I took the medical college admission test (MCAT) recently. The evening before the test, I went running—against my "better" judgment. The Toads were saying, "You need this time to study!" "You're not ready!" You have so much to stress about and be anxious over!" "This test could determine the rest of your life!" "What the heck are you doing taking a mindless run at a time like this?"

During my run, my attitude went through a metamorphosis. On the first lap I was agreeing with the Toads: I wasn't ready for the test…there was so much more to review…I wasn't smart enough to retain it…I didn't remember enough from my classes. I was sure I would bomb.

On the next lap I began to think about retaking the test if this one didn't go so well.

A few more laps and I began to focus on how well I had done on some practice tests, and—more importantly—how much I had improved with each practice test.

I felt some of the knots in my back begin to unwind, but the Toads were still there, telling me that this test was real, and would therefore be worse than the practice ones.

As I continued to run, I looked closely at strategies that had worked for me in the past, and the conditions under which I had taken the practice tests. I concentrated on relaxing. I told myself to focus on the material instead of what being right or wrong was going to lead to. It had nothing to do with the test itself and was only going to waste brain-power on extraneous stuff.

I worked out more "winning" strategies and began to convince myself that I would do well enough. By the end of the run, I was sure I would kick butt the next day, whatever they threw at me. I was ready!

When I finally got my scores from the MCAT, they were much higher than I expected. (This is one of the miracles that keeps me going back to the track!) Thank goodness I went for that run! In retrospect, I know I wouldn't have done nearly as well if I had taken all those Toads into the testing room with me.

Sometimes, I think I can even see Toads in other peoples' pockets, backpacks, and on their shoulders, whispering in their ears. Toads are everywhere.

I still have plenty of my own Toads, and new ones find me every day as I seek out new challenges. But killing Toads is now a regular part of my life, and the more I kill, the more I want to kill. Yesterday, I killed the "I-can't-seem-to-get-past-two-miles" Toad. I ran three miles in spite of a croaking chorus.

Section 4:
Toads at Work

Our doubts are traitors, and make us lose the good
we oft might win by fearing to attempt.
- *William Shakespeare*

Chapter 13

The Toad in Sheep's Clothing

Tony always dreamed of being a chef. With that in mind, restaurant work was all he ever did. He started out as a prep cook and worked his way to head cook. By his early twenties, he'd saved enough money to attend a well-respected school for the gourmet training he wanted. After that, he only worked in classier restaurants, eventually becoming a head chef. Over the years, he built an extensive repertoire of tasty, original dishes. The tall and lanky Tony had become highly respected among his peers.

Now, just before his fiftieth birthday, Tony was fulfilling a lifelong dream by opening his own restaurant. It was a nice place, not far from a military base on the west coast. Adding to Tony's thrill was the "partnership" aspect of having his daughter, Rana, onboard. She was the only family he had left after his wife died from cancer a year earlier.

Tall and slender and an artist in her own right, (a painter who had studied in Paris), Rana had beautiful blonde hair that framed her face like an award-winning portrait. But Rana was shy and preferred the solitude of a studio. She told Tony several times that she'd rather not work at the restaurant, but Tony persisted. He convinced her to be a server during lunches and be a hostess in the evenings. Despite her strong desire not to work in the restaurant, she never brought it up again. She didn't want to spoil her father's dream so soon after her mother's death.

Unbeknownst to Rana, a Sabotage Toad had jumped into her head, but hid its identity. It fooled her into wearing a pleasant demeanor, whispering for her to play the role of supportive daughter. But deep down the Toad was playing with Rana's mind.

"Tony's Place" opened on a warm day in May, and things went well. Tony spent a lot of time experimenting with new dishes, getting inventories established, and keeping the books.

But one thing Tony lacked was a head for marketing. All of his years had been spent in the kitchen. Rana's Sabotage Toad saw its chance. It whispered to her, "Forget marketing. Just serve good food and be pleasant." As a result, Rana told her dad that spending money on marketing was risky. She didn't believe promotions would draw more customers, it would just cost them money.

She never said these things to the employees, but behind the scenes Rana exerted a lot of influence on how Tony thought.

You can guess what happened. After a year of marginal growth, Tony's business slipped into a slow, steady decline. Not knowing what to do, Tony spent more time in the kitchen, growing skittish about spending money on advertising. The Toad had done its job: Tony now believed every penny was necessary for survival. He thought, "What if they spent money on advertising that didn't pay off? How would they pay their bills?"

One of the restaurant's regular customers was Steve, an experienced advertising and marketing consultant who regularly entertained clients at Tony's Place. When Tony learned what Steve did for a living, he picked his brain as to why more people weren't coming into the restaurant.

"It's definitely not because the food is bad," commented Steve. "This is by far the best food in town." The two men became friends. Steve wanted to see the restaurant succeed, so he took it upon himself to help Tony out in exchange for a few meals.

The first thing Steve did was design some discount coupons. "You need to print up a few thousand of these," Steve said.

Later that night, Tony showed the coupon to his daughter. "Oh my," she told him, "Every time someone uses one of those coupons we're going to lose money." Rana printed up only one hundred coupons. She convinced Tony that too many coupons would eat into their cash flow.

The next week when Steve came in for lunch with a client, Tony stopped by the table. "Those coupons didn't work," he said. Steve felt blindsided, especially in front of his client. After Tony walked away, Rana came over to the table to serve them. She was polite to Steve and thanked him for designing the coupons.

Over the next year, Steve offered Tony lots of solid marketing advice. Usually Tony loved the ideas, but he always came back to Steve a few days later with some restriction on what he had suggested. All along, Rana treated Steve with the utmost respect and courtesy, thanking him for his efforts.

The Sabotage Toad won its largest coup when Steve suggested advertising in the military base's newspaper. Tony liked the idea: a "two-for-one" Tuesday lunch special. Steve didn't wait: He placed the ad that day.

The morning the ad broke, Rana was concerned about how much money they were going to lose. She decided that the officers had enough money to buy lunch at full price, so the discount should go to enlisted soldiers only. Tony went along with her logic, but didn't say anything to Steve.

That Tuesday the restaurant was full for lunch. Rana was one of the servers, and she asked to see the military ID of everyone requesting the special. Several tables of officers got up and left in disgust when Rana told them the special was for enlisted soldiers only. A few officers pointed out that the ad mentioned no such restriction. Rana politely apologized, but they made loud comments of not ever coming back.

When Steve heard about this his jaw hit the floor. "Don't you want more business?" Tony parroted the logic his daughter presented him, but Steve couldn't believe his ears. It was unfathomable to him.

After this fiasco, Steve decided he couldn't help Tony anymore. He was a professional who knew how to bring in customers. Yet here, despite practically giving his services away, Tony wasn't enjoying the success Steve's other clients enjoyed. He felt he was fighting a losing war because all of his strategies were changed by the time they got to the front lines.

Steve stopped coming to Tony's Place. So did many others. Unknown to anyone, the Sabotage Toad had done its job.

On an unusually cold night in September, Tony hung the "Closed" sign on the door for the last time. A month later, Tony and his daughter moved to Kansas City where Tony took a job as executive chef at a nice restaurant and Rana spent a lot of time catching up on her painting. The Sabotage Toad, having done its work, then went out looking for another victim.

Thoughts on The Toad in Sheep's Clothing:

It's important here to remember that people are not Toads: They *have* Toads. And, although people may harbor and nourish Toads, they're not always conscious of it.

In this story, Rana was unable to set good boundaries and pursue her own calling. Then, when the Sabotage Toad took up residence, it invited its favorite buddy, the Passive-Aggressive Toad, and the two worked together flawlessly to achieve their aims. Rana wasn't even aware they were around.

Although it's hard to say without closer examination, Tony might have been feeding a Co-Dependent Toad. Although he was lonely after his wife's death, he should not have coerced his daughter (his last connection to his wife) into restaurant work, something God had not called her to do.

Tony also had a Short-Sighted Toad, which prevented him from seeing the long-term benefits of investing in marketing.

When two people are feeding Toads within themselves that feed off each other, a swirling vortex is created that keeps the Toads in a symbiotic relationship, making them hard to eliminate.

> Man's power of choice enables him to think
> like an angel or a devil, a king or a slave.
> Whatever he chooses, his mind will create and manifest.
> *- Frederick Bailes*

Chapter 14

Nancy's Dilemma

Nancy's story:

It was my third year in Las Vegas, studying hotel management at UNLV. To build my resume, I was working for a middle-grade hotel chain at a property just off the strip.

A husband and wife team managed the hotel, and Josh, their only son, also worked for them. His mom was the manager, his dad was the maintenance man. Josh's dad, Mr. Smythe (as he insisted we call him), was a rough man who barked orders as if he were crew chief on an oil rig. No tact! Sometimes even the customers received the brunt of his bark. He wasn't helping his business with that, even though he thought he sounded important.

Josh's mom made sure every employee knew she managed the place, and Josh, well, he was something special. At 23, he was quite immature, and had acquired a keen ability to tune out his parent's words, even though his parents nagged him constantly.

On one particular day, I heard Josh walk in the side door by the office. "Another day in the salt mines," I heard him mumble.

"Great," I thought. "Another workday with Mr. Wonderful. Well, I'll make the best of it." I was used to Josh being complacent and irresponsible. Working in a hotel was definitely *not* his cup of tea. He was there only because his parents owned the place. Besides, I was graduating next year so I took comfort in knowing he wouldn't be my coworker forever.

I was helping guests at the front desk when Josh walked up and stood next to me. Guests were lined up six deep, but he just stood there, watching me as if nobody else was in the lobby. I wanted to ask him to help, but his mom was beside me doing paperwork, and I didn't need to be scolded again for telling Josh what to do. "You're not his boss," his mom had told me on more than one occasion. So, I kept on helping guests as efficiently as I could.

After a few minutes, one of the guests walked into the lobby from our complimentary breakfast area. "You're out of coffee," he said. I smiled and said, "We'll be right there."

I knew better than to ask or tell Josh to go check. I turned to his mom and said, "We're out of coffee, and I'm helping customers here. Who would you like to refill the coffee?" It seemed childish, but that's how I had to get things done.

Josh's mom sighed without looking up. "Josh, go check the coffee," she said.

Josh copied her sigh, and I fought the desire to roll my eyes. What a Toad-filled family!

Josh walked around to the breakfast area, and I cringed when I heard him say, "You folks aren't supposed to be rummaging through the cupboards like that."

I thought to myself, "That's no way to talk to guests, Josh, and they wouldn't be rummaging through the cupboards if you would take some initiative and do your job!" But I kept my mouth shut.

Based on Josh's comment, I could just imagine the disaster in the breakfast area. I had been stuck behind the counter for almost an hour while Josh showed up late and his mom did paperwork. Customers were sitting down to wait for coffee as Josh walked off with the coffee pots. Ten minutes later he reappeared with coffee and then came back around and stood behind the front desk again. This time it was me who gave the heavy sigh.

Half an hour later, the front desk traffic died down enough for me to go check on the breakfast area. It was appalling—a total disaster. Plastic spoons were on the floor amidst spilled coffee and orange juice. The counter top was littered with sugar, coffee stirrers, empty creamer packets, and more spilled coffee and orange juice. The napkin holders were both empty, and so was the container for plastic ware. No cereal bowls were available. Glancing to the food items, I noted that the cold cereal was almost empty, as were the jelly packets and the cinnamon rolls. I looked for Styrofoam cups and found none.

Inside I was pretty miffed at Josh, who wasn't doing anything but standing around. "What is that boy's problem?" I thought.

I decided to let Josh and his mom handle the front desk. In ten short minutes, I restocked and cleaned the breakfast area so it looked fresh and ready to go, just like it did at 5:00 a.m. "What is so hard about this?" I thought.

Just then Mr. Smythe came into the breakfast area. "This area closes in ten minutes!" he barked. "Get what you need and get out." The guests looked up in astonishment, and I cringed in embarrassment. I instantly revisited my internal debate about finding another job. "Then I would be free from these Toads!" But I needed to show job longevity on my resume. Oh, what a dilemma!

Thoughts on Nancy's Dilemma:

It appears that quite a few Toads existed in Josh's family. It's likely that Josh was in a vortex of systemic family Toads, and it showed in his work ethic. Is it possible that Josh managed to squirm through life by getting by with the bare minimum wherever he went? If so, Josh has a very hard road ahead of him in life.

Josh's parents have quite the diversified Toad collection: Control Toads, Complacent Toads, Barking Toads, Ignoring Toads, and probably the ever unpopular Task-Only Toads, where people skills are left out of the picture for the purpose of completing a task.

On the other hand, Nancy has a good grasp of what Toads are and how they prevent forward motion. Hats off to Nancy.

A failure is not a mistake, it may simply be the best one can do under the circumstances. The real mistake is to stop trying.
                                    - B. F. Skinner

Chapter 15

The Toad in the Piano

(A Toad Funeral)

Dressed to elegant perfection, Julie, a professional pianist affiliated with the symphony orchestra in her city, was accompanying a tenor for his master's degree recital. The audience was over two hundred music professors and graduate musician students at a major university in California. The selection, by Brahms, was a dramatic story of star-crossed lovers who are separated but then united at the end. A challenging piece both technically and artistically, the pianist and tenor were giving exemplary performances. Everything went without blemish until the very last of the sixteen songs, when perfection was ruined at the last second: Julie hit a wrong note on the final chord.

Mortified, Julie immediately corrected the chord, but the mistake was obvious and glaring, especially in front of a musically informed audience. She stared at the face of the now silent piano as the audience gave polite applause. What would she do now? She was a professional who played with the city's symphony orchestra! What would become of her reputation?

She envisioned a saw coming up through the stage floor, sawing a circle around her so she would fall through it and be taken away from this site of utter embarrassment. An otherwise flawless performance had been marred by a singular, glaring mistake.

Her next performance, a violin and piano recital, was only a week away. What could she do? She was under contract and she had to perform. Would she once again flub the final note and ruin someone else's recital? A Toad of Doubt grew in her mind until it took over her entire waking life. It sat there, chipping away at her confidence, waiting for her defenses to weaken for even a second. Then it filled her thoughts with mind-numbing anxiety.

Julie, herself a doctoral student, took her fear of yet another public humiliation to one of her professors. He told her not to worry, and suggested that she take beta-blockers, a drug to relieve anxiety. He assured her that many professional musicians dealt with their performance fears by taking drugs. He confided that this is what he did to deal with his own performance anxiety.

She considered his suggestion briefly. It would make her life much easier. However, after thinking it through, she refused to avoid the Toad in that way. She felt that it was cheating—that performing artists need to learn how to face and deal with their Toads. She wanted to face her particular Toad with a clear, albeit frightened, mind.

Going into her next performance, Julie was extremely nervous. She kept envisioning that last chord where she would hit a wrong note. During the entire recital, she did fine, until that last note when her hand came down on the keys to make the final sound. She felt the hesitation in her downward stroke. Her fingers hit the keys a bit too slowly. Although the chord was correct, she knew that she had artistically failed. The Toad had impeded the optimal flow of her performance.

The mistake was not really noticeable, except to her. She had managed, through the force of her will, to push her fearful mind past the weight, power, and will of the Toad. It had tried to trip her up on that final chord, but she pushed back and suppressed that little demon. It wasn't perfect, but it wasn't a glaring mistake. Inside, Julie felt like she had gained back some ground.

Julie's next performance was a little easier—and the one after that was even easier. Eventually, the Toad of Doubt died by way of starvation. All that remained within Julie were her normal performance jitters.

Editor's Note:

Looking back, Julie wondered what would have happened if her contract hadn't compelled her to perform again so soon after that single, but glaring mistake. She was so embarrassed that she even thought about quitting music altogether to avoid the power of that Toad.

And powerful it was, for it had taken over her mind and filled her thoughts with self-doubt. If left to grow, it might have become a permanent crippling force. However, Julie did the right thing. She faced it and conquered it soon after its emergence.

Julie, now a piano teacher, tells her students about that Toad and how she faced and killed it. First of all, it helps her students understand that she is not infallible, that such events are part of being a performance artist. Most importantly, it teaches her students that being a professional means having the character and courage to deal with one's Toads without denial or drugs.

Finish each day and be done with it. You have done what you could.
Some blunders and absurdities no doubt creep in;
forget them as soon as you can.
- *Ralph Waldo Emerson*

Chapter 16

A Matter of Focus

(A Toad Funeral)

Marshall's story:

It was 2:29 in the morning. I had locked the liquor doors a half-hour ago, and the 7-11 store where I worked the night shift was now quiet. Beer and wine were the big sellers in the wee hours of the morning, but after 2:00 a.m., when all alcohol sales had to stop according to state law, store traffic always slowed to a crawl.

I was between jobs and looking for a new direction, so I had taken a night shift position to lay low. I needed to regroup from my recent divorce and decide where I wanted to go with my life.

At 24 with no kids, I had been living the party life, but after my wife left me for my best friend, I decided it was time to grow up.

The university was only two miles away, and I'd been thinking about going back to school to get a degree in engineering. Or maybe firefighting. My dad was a fire fighter, and if I chose to follow in my father's footsteps it might be a signal to my parents that I was finally "coming around."

With no one in the store, I was taking a short break to read an article in *Popular Science* before starting in on the nightly clean up and restocking ritual when a sandy-haired, blue eyed kid walked in. I

67

made my way back behind the counter and continued reading the magazine article.

A minute later the blonde young man walked up to the counter with a six pack of soda and set it on the counter. Instinctively I straightened up and started ringing up the six-pack without even looking at the customer. "Will that be all for you?" I asked, out of routine. As I looked up, the young man was pointing a gun straight at me. "Open the register," he said.

"Oh gosh," I thought, "this kid can't be more than 17 or 18 years old!" I stared at the kid with disbelief. This wasn't happening!

"Open the register!" yelled the kid. I didn't want to give him any money, but I didn't want to get shot, either. I figured if he was going to get any money, he'd have to take it himself. I pushed the key on the register that opened the drawer and stepped back away from the drawer with my hands up at shoulder height. "If you want the money," I said, "you take it."

The kid raised the revolver up into my face. It was so close I could see the bullets in their chambers. "Get on the floor!" he yelled. I turned, got down on my knees and started to get on the floor. Every second seemed an eternity. I thought about all that I'd done wrong in life and how I wished I'd done things differently. I thought about my failed marriage, losing my previous job, all the fights with my parents, everything. I thought about fishing with my dad, and never being able to catch anything decent. My mind raced. I had a sinking feeling that the cold tile floor of a 7-11 store would be the last thing I'd ever see while on the earth. I could hear the kid taking the money from the cash drawer, and since I had seen the robber's face, I figured it was mere moments before a bullet would enter my brain and either end my life or make me a permanent vegetable.

It got quiet, and I couldn't tell what the robber was doing. Was he stealing lottery tickets? Taking cigarettes? I felt tortured, waiting there to be killed.

Suddenly I heard a voice. "Are you okay?"

The voice belonged to an older man, not the robber, and I wasn't sure what to do. "Are you okay?" the man asked again.

I slowly moved my head around and looked up. "What are you doing on the floor?" the man asked. I stood up shaking, and told him I had just been robbed. "I think I'm going to have to ask you to leave the store," I said.

After calling the police and my manager, I tried to collect my wits. My manager came in and reviewed the security videotape with the police, and then told me I'd done a good job. I thought otherwise. I knew store rules stated that I was supposed to cooperate totally with the robber, and treat the robbery just like any other transaction. But I had resisted, and in so doing, risked my life. I couldn't get the sight of that revolver out of my mind. I had done so many things wrong.

My manager stayed and helped me with the rest of the night shift work, which I appreciated. He offered to let me have a few nights off, but I told him that the next night was my regular night off and I thought I'd be okay.

The next morning I crawled into bed at 8:30 am, which was my routine after getting off the night shift. Just as I was dozing off to sleep, I sat straight up in bed, gasping for breath, I had just dreamt about the revolver pointed in my face. Ten minutes later, the same thing happened again. Over and over, throughout the morning and into the afternoon, I woke up every ten or fifteen minutes because of that gun in my face. Obviously, I didn't get much sleep. Thank God I had the next night off.

Tired of that recurring, heart-pounding dream, I got up and went for a walk. I couldn't stop thinking that I hadn't followed company procedures and it almost cost me my life. Maybe if I'd just been more alert instead of reading the magazine I wouldn't have been held up.

Back in my apartment that night I was exhausted from no sleep. Eventually, by midnight, I started dozing, but I kept waking up every ten minutes, dreaming about a gun being stuck in my face.

No matter what I tried to focus on, I kept dreaming about that stupid gun. So the next day, after two days of no sleep, I called my grandfather who lived a few miles away. I needed *something*. Even sleeping pills weren't helping.

At Grandpa's house, I told him about the robbery and how I couldn't sleep because of this recurring dream. "I just keep thinking how much I screwed up," I told him.

"You gotta stop letting this eat at you from the inside," Grandpa said. "I hear you saying how you did things wrong. You've got a voice in your head telling you what you did wrong and it's blocking you from focusing on what you did right."

I didn't say anything, but I must have looked puzzled because Grandpa continued.

"If I'm not mistaken, those stores have a policy for what to do in case of a robbery, right?" I nodded. "Okay," he said, "tonight when you're back to work, find that list of things to do and write down everything you did right. Don't focus on what you didn't do—focus on what you did right and make me a list."

I didn't have any better ideas, so I followed Grandpa's advice. After things slowed down at work that night I pulled out the store policy for what to do during a robbery and made a list of things I'd done right. To my surprise, my list of what I had done right was a whole lot longer than what I had done wrong. I felt better almost immediately.

The next day I got off work at 7:00 a.m. and headed straight home to sleep. And sleep I did! I slept from 8 in the morning until 9 at night, never once waking up with any nightmares. Well-rested, I went back to work the next night at 11 p.m. and enjoyed myself the whole night through.

The next morning I called Grandpa. I told him that his assignment had done the trick and that I'd slept like a baby with no nightmares. "Keep it up," he told me. "Stay focused on what you're doing right."

And that's what I do now. Whenever that little voice of self-criticism tries to take over, I now know how to shut it up.

Section 5:
Tools for Toad Killers

Good judgment comes from experience;
Experience comes from bad judgment.
- *Author Unknown*

Chapter 17

Gain Experience

One of the best ways to enhance our Toad-elimination skills is to gain experience. The more experience we have under our belts, the easier it is to recognize (and then eliminate) the Toads trying to slow us down! But it's important to know that gaining experience is not as simple as having something happen to you. When we break down the word *experience* into its different parts, we learn what it *really* means to gain experience. Therefore, a little background on the composition of this word may prove helpful.

In ancient Persia, there were stories about malevolent spirits that lurked in the forests. Whenever people were so unlucky as to encounter one, they could get hurt, maybe crippled, and, sometimes, even die. An evil spirit was known as a "peri." That word jumped over to the Greek language, and, from there, to Latin. The word "peri" now forms the root of such words as peril, perish, expert, and experience.

When we break down the word into its specific parts we get a better sense of what it really means:

    ex   "out of" or "from"
    peri   "test" or "danger"
    ence   "action" or "condition" or "quality"

73

Thus, etymologically, the word "experience" means *to get through a dangerous situation*. It does not mean to possess a certain body of knowledge, as is a common misuse today. Experience, in the true sense of the word, indicates the accumulation of wisdom from having faced and, most importantly, worked through, perilous or risky actions. I'm not saying we should all go bungee jumping or sky diving, but without facing at least a modicum of emotional stress that accompanies being outside our comfort zone, it's hard to gain experience, and following that, wisdom.

While we're digging into the meaning of words, allow me to point out that an *expert*, regardless of paper credentials, is by definition, someone who has gained experience. Too often people say someone is an expert if they have a lot of "book learning," but the word really refers to someone with actual, real-world experience.

So how do we gain experience? The simple answer is we have to get out there and live life! We need to expose ourselves to situations and be willing to make mistakes. Then, with the wisdom we gain from having experience, we have a much easier time recognizing Toads and dealing with them in a courageous and healthy way.

I love the following axiom, not only because it contains a tasty morsel of humor, but mainly because it contains a significant serving of truth:

> Good judgment comes from experience.
> Experience comes from bad judgement.

Now, bad judgment is not required to gain experience, but this statement is a wonderful way of saying we have to get out there and deal with things outside our comfort zone. It acknowledges that we're going to make mistakes along the way (bad judgment), but that we're going to gain experience from those mistakes (get through dangerous situations), and then, as a result, be able to make better decisions (have good judgment). The following story illustrates the concept:

A man was working at a large corporation, overseeing a high-profile project. One day he made a huge mistake which ended up costing his company more than a million dollars. Embarrassed beyond compare, the man could hardly muster the nerve to come to work after that.

Early the next week the man was called into the president's office, and he feared the worst. After the man was seated, the president started explaining a new, cutting-edge project that he thought would take the company to new heights. The man thought the president might have been confused about which meeting he was in, especially when the president said to him, "and I'd like you to oversee this new project."

Flustered, the man replied, "I'm not sure I understand. I'm the one who made that huge mistake last week that cost the company over a million dollars. Didn't you call me in here to fire me?"

The president laughed in response, saying, "Fire you? Why on earth would I do that? I just spent a million dollars training you!"

The president knew that the experience of that huge mistake would enable the man to recognize Toads much better, and prevent them from entering into future projects. And, similar to the president, we, too, must develop judgment about who else has and has not gained experience. This usually comes as we gain experience ourselves, for then we are better able to recognize who else has it, too.

This is pretty much a no-brainer if you already have a lot of miles behind you, but if you've not been out-and-about in the world much, it's wise to learn how to identify who has or does not have experience. Just because someone is a nice person doesn't mean they've learned how to navigate difficult situations. Discerning who has/doesn't have experience helps when you're deciding who might be able to help you in removing a Toad, and also how much assistance is needed from you when you're helping them do the same.

Just remember that experience has to be gained. Learning has to be constructed. Some people can stumble into situations from now until Doomsday and not learn anything from them.

To identify someone with experience, listen to a person's language. Is it victim language, or does it speak of lessons learned? And if it speaks of true lessons learned, has the person built and maintained initiative, or is their language full of reasons to "avoid?" Your answers to these questions will let you know whether or not you're dealing with someone with true experience.

With all this mind, I hope you can see why it's important that we learn from our own predicaments. If we regularly avoid difficult situations, we lose opportunities to learn from them, and we remain unequipped to kill certain Toads. This is not to say we should look for trouble. Rather, when problems do arise, we gain experience when we face the troubles and actually work through them.

We can also learn from the experiences of others. Read about the lives of people. Listen to their dilemmas. Ask people to elaborate when they talk about how they worked through their struggles. The recognized value of stories is why this book includes a wide variety of "Toad stories." We can learn much from the experiences of others. The more stories we know about the different kinds of Toads people face and how those Toads can be dealt with, the easier it will be for us to recognize our own Toads and rid ourselves of them.

Granted, learning from stories does not give us first-hand experience, but we can and do learn from what we hear and read. This is especially true of stories with strong emotional factors, because when learning is tied to emotions, it "sticks" better.

In western society, narrative learning in education and narrative therapy in psychology are growing movements, and ministers continue to use stories today just like Jesus used parables some 2000 years ago. Stories help us perceive the patterns of ourselves, and are excellent tools for helping us construct meaning.

Bottom line, you definitely want to gain experience for yourself, but you can also learn from hearing about other people's experiences. The learning you gain from your own and others' experiences will help you recognize and eradicate Toads, especially the systemic ones that like to remain hidden from our everyday awareness.

Friendship is the process of refining the
truths we can tell one another.
- *Adrienne Rich*

Chapter 18

Establish True Friendships

It is hard for us to see our own Toads. This truth is illustrated in a line from Joseph Heller's best-selling novel, *Catch 22*:

You can't see the flies in your eyes if
you have flies in your eyes.

Therefore, a powerful tool for Toad killers is to establish true friendships. Friends can help us spot the Toads hiding and lurking in our minds. And, if we're smart, we let our friends help us.

Even the Mayo Clinic devotes attention to the benefits of having friends. Some of the benefits they list for having friends are:

- Increases your sense of purpose and belonging
- Boosts you happiness / reduces stress
- Improves self-confidence and self-worth

With this list, we can see that having friends is good for Toad killing. A sense of purpose helps propel you toward your goals, and that momentum helps minimize Toads (see chapter 22, *Setting Goals*). Reducing stress allows you to devote the energy needed for killing Toads (see chapter 23 for other ways to relieve stress). And self-confidence is a very helpful asset when tackling any Toad.

If a friend approaches you about a Toad that might be slowing you down, remember that it's in your best interest to hear it out and give consideration to your friend's comments. Yes, it may be painful to hear, but sometimes the truth does hurt. As it says in the book of Proverbs, "Faithful are the wounds of a friend; but the kisses of an enemy are deceitful" (Pr. 27:6). A true friend has your best interests at heart.

Even though your friend may truly want to help, it's quite possible you'll get defensive when you're first approached. In fact, you may even choose to ignore that one friend's comments, thinking you don't have the Toad. However, if someone else makes similar observations about you, well ... you may actually have the Toad!

Just remember that having true friendships also means being a true friend, and that can be difficult at times. If someone is trying to hide from a Toad, say, perhaps a drinking problem, and you collude with that denial, then you are an enabler, not a friend.

As the quote from Adrienne Rich points out at the top of this chapter, good friends are those who can safely point out Toads to each other. Following that, good friends also help find ways to turn Toads into carcasses. But friendship at that level requires trust, so one of the best things we can do to build good friendships is to be trustworthy, and choose as friends other people who do the same. Too often we call people "friends" who really are only buddies or acquaintances (Facebook has not helped with this tendency). Therefore, be careful about who you choose as true friends. After all, we don't want to discuss our Toads with just anybody!

As you may know, it can be easy to see Toads in other people. Sometimes too easy. This is especially true if someone has upset us, if we're insecure, or if we have a reason for distrust. Sometimes, we can even see Toads that aren't there! For this reason we should be cautious: We are responsible for our perceptions. If we construct imaginary Toads in other people, that says more about us than them.

On the other hand, sometimes it is hard to see Toads in our friends. At least two reasons exist for this:

1. We don't want to risk the static of pointing them out.
2. It says something about us if we have Toad-filled friends.

As you may have discerned, a core principle in this chapter is that being a Toad killer is a two-way street. We can't be selfish about it. We must work not only to eliminate Toads from our own lives, but also help our close friends be free of their Toads, too. Obviously, we must accept others and ourselves as people who have Toads, but it's not exactly healthy to stand by and let ourselves or our friends be diminished by Toads. As previously mentioned, dealing with Toads can be painful, therefore, one key to success in the endeavor of Toad killing is using tact.

Foundationally, pointing out a Toad to a friend requires creating an emotionally safe environment. After all, nobody truly enjoys hearing negative things about themselves. And it's important to remember that people are *not* Toads, people *have* Toads!

When you start talking about a Toad in someone else's life, you may want to start by bringing up how the Toad seems to be holding that person back. Tell about situations you've observed, and how you think the Toad had an impact on the outcome of those situations. It's very important to be objective, not personal. In other words, speak to events, not the person. And using Toad language takes the onus off the person and puts it on the Toad, thus making your friend feel safer (aka not personally criticized).

Here are examples of the various ways people might approach someone with an Anger Toad. Let's call them good, better, and best, even though "good" is not so good:

Good: "When you were talking with John you got very angry."

Better: "I noticed during the conversation with John the other day that the anger was palpable."

Best: "I noticed during the conversation with John the other day, an Anger Toad was egging you on."

The first option really isn't all that good, because it's very easy for someone hearing that to take it personally. The wording literally says, "You got angry." Because the concepts of angry and anger are easily blurred, the phrase is easily heard as, "You *became* anger." Nobody wants that. "Becoming anger" makes one a bad person. Because your friend is not a bad person, this really isn't a good approach.

The second option is much better, and resembles something a counselor might say. It's talking about the problem from an objective perspective. However, the third option is best, because the Toad language completely removes the anger from the person and places it on a Toad. With that framework, your friend and you can talk about things easily and objectively, without much chance of your friend getting defensive and shutting down. From there, you simply help your friend find alternative behaviors in a matter-of-fact dialog.

However, no matter how you approach someone about a Toad, friends may start getting defensive. If that happens, I suggest backing down to allow for a little venting. Here are three good things to do if that happens:

- Keep quiet and pay attention
- Show love and concern in your facial expression, not disagreement or judgment
- After the other person calms down, paraphrase what the person says without agreeing or disagreeing

Showing this level of patience can be difficult, but it is part of what good friends do. If the friendship has any kind of mutual trust at all, the truth – and forward progress – will eventually win out.

Finally, don't be too defensive yourself, for we all have Toads (Where else do all of our warts come from?). Like Coach Hatfield says, "We all have Toads, and that's okay." Many Toads simply make us a little quirky. But we should learn how to help kill the ones that cripple and diminish the potential in us and in our friends, and ask them to do the same for us. True friends help us recognize—and eliminate—our Toads.

You are a product of your environment, so choose the environment
that will best develop you toward your objective.
- *W. Clement Stone*

Chapter 19

Be Aware of Your Environment

Recall the questions asked of Mr. Centipede by the Toad. "How do you walk with all those legs in perfect unison? How in the world do you manage to move them all, much less at the same time?" These are reasonable questions that could have been asked out of intellectual curiosity. Regardless, Mr. Centipede's mind put the questions into a feedback loop that resulted in paralysis.

In actuality, we don't know whether or not the Toad had evil or disruptive intent with his questioning. Some Toads aim their weapons out in the open, others are good at camouflaging their evil intent, and some things we attribute to Toads that may not be Toads at all.

The same is true in the people around us. While our adversaries may assail us with Toady rhetoric, our best friends and loving family members will occasionally ask us questions like, "What compelled you to do that?" Coming from someone we don't trust, that question could be a trap. But coming from friends and concerned family members, the question could be genuine and safe. Yet at the same time, our friends and parents may be the caretakers of Toads.

For this reason, we need to be aware of our environment. We need to be aware of how we're perceiving information, processing information, and making decisions – both our mental and our physical environments.

81

Mental Environment

Internally, we need to choose what we listen to and how we listen to it. The responsibility for our mental life is always our own. As an acquaintance of mine is fond of saying, "Growing old is mandatory, growing up is optional." It's cute, but it's a cop-out. Conversely, when the apostle Paul was teaching about personal responsibility, he said, "When I was young, I spoke as a child and acted as a child. Now that I have grown, I have put off childish things."

The underlying truth in his statement is that, as adults, we are totally responsible for how we perceive and process our own thoughts. As described in chapter 12, *Running Through the Toads*, we can think of Toads as sitting on our shoulders and whispering in our ears. It's one thing to hear a thought in our heads, it's something different to entertain it. A self-defeating thought does not deserve a cocktail party, a BBQ, or even a cup of coffee. Don't let such thoughts hang around and gain a foothold. When you hear a thought that doesn't resonate with what you know is true in your spirit, send it packing!

Physical Environment

Again, recall that even though people may behave in Toady ways, people themselves are never Toads, people *have* Toads. Therefore, we should be in touch with our intuition about people. Some pack a lot of Toads, and others not so many.

When we're around Toad-filled people, we can slip and take things personally, or we can remain objective. To give yourself the greatest chance at remaining objective, it's best if you've established principled standards for how you want to respond to nonsense. A good career- or life-coach can help you with establishing such standards.

Being aware of your surroundings is like being a good hunter. Deer hunters will tell you that when hunting, they don't really look for deer—they look for something different in the environment. Aside from obvious indicators like tracks and scat, they're looking for other factors: Broken twigs appearing on low-hanging branches; the sound of a hoof hitting a fallen log; bushes that "rustle" in a direction opposite the wind. Deer don't always walk out and say, "Here I am."

The same principle applies to Toad hunting. Therefore, pay attention to your environment and notice when something is different around you. In so doing, you increase the likelihood of identifying and removing Toads that can hold you back.

The following is a non-exhaustive list of possible indicators that Toads are lurking within you or nearby:

Personal Indicators:

Non-specific anxiety

A habit of defensiveness

A sense of depression

Loss of sense of humor

Inefficiency

Inability to relax

Loss of sociability

Lack of passion

Feeling insignificant

Habitual resentment

Frequent fear or anger

Low energy levels

Habit of procrastination

Inability to sleep

Chronic back tension

Withdrawal from others

Lack of enthusiasm

Fear of solitude

Social Indicators:

A deep sense of distrust

A sense of victimhood

Reduced productivity

Negative synergy

Lack of cooperation

A stressed atmosphere

Not feeling part of the team

Undue hesitation

Lethargy

A "CYA" mentality

Tense conversations

Excuses & Scapegoating

Lack of laughter

A bureaucratic culture

Lack of shared vision

Excessive wariness

If any of these indicators appear in your life, they may point to the presence of Toads. If you identify any such signs, get ready for a Toad hunt! You don't even have to shoot them. If you see a Fear Toad trying to block your path, just step on him, squish him, and keep on moving!

People of genius do not excel in a profession because they
work in it, they work in it because they excel in it.
- *William Hazlett*

Chapter 20

Identify Your Vocation

Doing something you are not designed to do is fertile ground for the emergence of Toads. This truth was illustrated in chapter 13, *The Toad in Sheep's Clothing*, where a woman worked in a restaurant when she was meant to be an artist. The ripple-effect of that action may have cost her father his dream.

In his book, *Let Your Life Speak: Listening for the Voice of Vocation*, Parker Palmer says, "the pilgrimage toward true self will take time, many places, and years."

Pay attention to the fit between your essential self and your situations. If what you are doing doesn't get easier and easier, that indicates what you are doing does not fit God's design for you. We are designed to continually grow, to increase our competence and connection to our chosen endeavor, and to become ever more capable of facing new challenges. If these things are not true in your career, then you may be doing the wrong thing.

As a former San Diego Teacher of the Year commented at a workshop some years ago:

> The first ten years I went to school in the morning all enthusiastic and then trudged home in the afternoon feeling like a drained battery. Now, it's the reverse, I go to school to get reinvigorated.

That statement tells us that the teacher realized he was doing what God meant for him to do, even if it took him a few years to figure it out! Along these same lines, we can consider this story about a little-known dancer:

Just before it was time for the dance she had rehearsed for months, something had hold of her legs, saying, "Don't do this. Don't go out there and perform this dance. Do something else."

But she was supposed to dance! Still, the voice came forth within her again, louder and louder. The voice spoke confidently, sure of its connection to her essential self. And the voice was completely free of Toads.

For years she had trained herself as a dancer and had identified herself as an entertainer who danced. This night was the night her career was to begin: Amateur night at the Harlem Opera House. Her dance was on the schedule. Her routine was rehearsed. The music was in place. But there was a voice saying she shouldn't do it—she was not supposed to dance for all these people. The voice was actually telling her to sing. She felt it in her very essence. In the acorn of her soul and in the whole of her potential, she was a singer, not a dancer.

When the emcee announced to the audience that she was going to dance for them, she shyly but bravely caught his attention.

"Yes young lady? Oh! Pardon me. Miss Ella Fitzgerald has decided not to dance for us. She will sing for us instead."

Four encores later, Ella Fitzgerald began her career as one of this nation's musical treasures. She could have easily mistaken that voice as a Toad trying to stop her from success. Perhaps she had a relationship with God and could sense His guiding hand. Regardless, by listening to the voice of her vocation, she changed the world of music forever.

If you are unaware of your calling and would like a little guidance, you might consider completing an *Interest Inventory* or a *Career Planning Assessment*. The latter is an online assessment available through my company, Workplace-Excellence.com.

To shun one's cross makes it heavier.
- Henri Frederic Amiel

Chapter 21

Take Responsibility

Don't accept self-defeating behavior in yourself; you can do better. Don't wallow in self-pity; many people are worse off than you. Accept boredom as a personal responsibility; any mind that finds boredom in itself is one lacking imagination or curiosity. Watch out for narcissism, as some people like to focus on their own issues and woes. So what to do? Go out the door and help someone in some way. There is no greater gift to yourself.

As the late Stephen Covey said in his book *The Seven Habits of Highly Effective People*:

> Look at the word responsibility—"response-ability"—the ability to choose your response. Highly proactive people recognize their responsibility. They don't blame circumstances, conditions, or conditioning for their behavior. Their behavior is a product of their conscious choice, based on values, rather than a product of their conditions, based on feeling.

Self-defeating behavior, like a Victim Toad, seeks to make you a victim, unable to respond in ways that bring you fulfillment. No matter the situation, we each have a choice to engage or disengage. Disengaging from unhealthy situations – or choosing to engage in healthy ones – are ways of taking responsibility.

87

Too many people complain of the doldrums, finding nothing to do but what they've always done. Or, they describe it as being stuck, beating their heads against the walls of their circumstances and feeling trapped in their situations. They're imprisoned in the status quo and they don't like it. Toads, however, do.

In his book, *Do One Thing Different*, Bill O'Hanlon advises us to develop a solution-oriented approach. He comments:

> Whenever you are stuck with a problem, try something new. Do something—just one thing—different. Break the pattern of the problem. Insanity is doing the same thing over and over again and expecting different results!

Mechanics know that having the right tool makes all the difference when trying to get something done. Hence, they're not afraid to get a different tool if what they're using at the time is not effective. In the same way, if what you're doing is not getting you past a bothersome Toad, consider trying something else. Some folks call this "thinking outside the box."

If you're having a tough time thinking of alternatives, ask a friend, but be careful! Don't rationalize why your friend's input won't work. Give it serious consideration, and try it! Doing something differently can be awkward, and may not even work. However, if nothing else, a different approach stretches our minds and opens our eyes to new ways of getting around the Toads holding us back.

Bill O'Hanlon tells a story in his book that illustrates the power of "doing one thing different":

> A favorite aunt of one of Milton Erickson's (a psychologist) colleagues was living in Milwaukee and had become quite seriously depressed. When Erickson gave a lecture there, the colleague asked him to visit the aunt and see if he could help her. The woman had inherited a fortune and lived in the family mansion. But she lived all alone, never having married, and by now had lost most of her close relatives. She was in her sixties and had medical problems that put her in a wheelchair and

severely curtailed her social activities. She had begun to hint to her nephew that she was thinking of suicide.

O'Hanlon tells how Erickson visited the colleague's aunt and found her depressed and isolated. She had previously been an avid church-goer, but since being confined to a wheelchair, she now went only on Sunday. The woman had only one joy in her life; a greenhouse nursery attached to the house. The aunt had a green thumb and her best hours were spent growing flowers. She was particularly fond of African violets.

The woman admitted to Erickson that her depression had become quite serious. His unique approach was to suggest she "do one thing different".

O'Hanlon continues:

> Erickson told her that he thought depression was not really the problem. It was clear to him that she was not being a very good Christian. She was taken aback by this and began to bristle, until he explained, "Here you are with all this money, time on your hands, and a green thumb. And it's all going to waste. What I recommend is that you get a copy of your church membership list and then look in the latest church bulletin. You'll find announcements of births, illnesses, graduations, engagements, and marriages in there – all the happy and sad events in the lives of people in the congregation. Make a number of African violet cuttings and get them well established. Then repot them in gift pots and have your handyman drive you to the homes of people who are affected by these happy or sad events. Bring them a plant and your congratulations or condolences and comfort, whichever is appropriate to the situation."

Hearing this, the woman agreed that perhaps she had fallen down in her Christian duty and agreed to do more.

Twenty years later as I [Bill O'Hanlon] was sitting in Erickson's office, he pulled out one of his scrapbooks and showed me an article from the *Milwaukee Journal*. It was a

89

feature article with a large headline that read, *"African Violet Queen of Milwaukee Dies, Mourned by Thousands."* The article detailed the life of this incredibly caring woman who had become famous for her trademark flowers and her charitable work with people in the community for the ten years preceding her death.

With this story, O'Hanlon informs us that either "changing the viewing" or "changing the doing" of a problem in even one way can change the situation dramatically. I hasten to add that it can also kill Toads. Erickson's insight helped the woman kill the Toads of Depression and Isolation that were growing within her.

Bottom line, choosing to do something differently than the way you've been doing it can sometimes be enough to get past a Toad blocking your way.

If you don't know where you are going,
you might wind up someplace else.
- Yogi Berra

Chapter 22

Set Goals

Toads do not thrive well in environments filled with initiative (Most Toads do not like movement). The thing to member here is this: Initiative is toxic to Toads.

Therefore, one way to defeat Toads is to build momentum by setting goals and working to accomplish those goals. You may need to start small, but a list of goals creates a caravan of initiatives that is focused and on the move. And, initiative begets initiative.

With "The Big Mo" on your side, Toads will rarely show themselves. And, when they do, because of your momentum they are more easily identified and shoved aside. After all, momentum is a powerful force! You become a team unto yourself, and you will also attract people who wish to contribute to your enterprise, whatever it may be.

Psychologists often call this "flow," and its power is phenomenal. Just ask any basketball player who ever tried to put a Toad in the head of Michael Jordan or LeBron James.

Since goals allow us to create momentum, a chapter on goal setting is appropriate. The main concepts as well as the details of goal setting are taught in myriad workshops by consultants and trainers worldwide. Plus, other books specialize on the topic. So, for this book, my goal is simply to give you an overview.

Before goals are set, it is important to identify one's vision. A vision is a direction for one's life (personally), or a direction for an organization (professionally). Simply stated, a vision statement identifies the general direction you want to go. If you like, you can also write a mission statement, which provides a general outline of what you will do en route to achieving your vision.

Goals, on the other hand, are one-time achievable activities that lead us in the direction of our vision and help us on our mission. The three work together like this:

Vision: The direction in which we're going

Mission: What you'll do to get where you're going

Goals: Clearly defined, realistic, measurable actions that support the mission and have a deadline.

When writing goals, I advocate using the S.M.A.R.T. acronym:

S – Specific. Clear and easy to understand.

M – Measurable. How long? How far? How many?

A – Action-Oriented. A verb that dictates our action.

R – Realistic. Is it sensible, rational, and practical?

T – Time-of-Completion. Goals must have deadlines.

The most neglected component of goal setting is assigning a Time-of-Completion. Consequently, many excellent ideas are never realized simply because no deadlines were created.

Even when deadlines are created, too often it's rush-rush-rush in the final minutes and hours. Perhaps you've heard the phrase, "If it wasn't for the last minute, nothing would get done." That's because Procrastination Toads slow us down. For that reason, I advocate creating mini-goals – milestones or checkpoints – to balance out the workload. This helps keep Procrastination Toads in check, because they thrive when no deadlines are set.

Laura Crawshaw, a longtime associate and founder of the Executive Insight Development Group, is fond of asking her clients, "By when?" She asks this so often that I associate her with that question! Laura understands the fundamental importance of including a time-of-completion whenever setting a goal.

Let me also emphasize that goals must be realistic. Undemanding goals fail to challenge us. Completing undemanding goals is unfulfilling and can lead to an apathetic mindset. Just ask any kid who's bored in school. On the other hand, goals set too hard lead to discouragement and grudging compliance.

Here are a few quick examples of good and not-so-good goal statements:

Not so good example – I want to make more money.

The statement is not specifically measurable (how much is more?), lacks a clear specific action ("making" money is illegal – perhaps "earn" or "save" is better?), contains no time of completion (no "by when?), and we don't know if it's realistic because we don't know how much. Essentially, "I want to make more money" is a mission, not a goal.

<u>Good example</u> – I will save $4,000 before August 1, 20XX.

$4,000 is measurable. *Save* is a specific action. *Before August 1, 20XX* (you name the year) is a specific time of completion. It meets the S.M.A.R.T. standards. Setting S.M.A.R.T. Goals gives us momentum.

Another reason I emphasize setting goals is because doing so focuses us on where we want to go, and we always move in the direction of our focus. This is powerful, so it bears repeating:

We move in the direction of our focus.

As an example of this, in my younger years, when I would be riding my bicycle up a hill with a long incline, I would often watch the pavement ahead of my front tire as I concentrated my energy on getting up the hill. Occasionally a rock would be in the path of my

93

tire. I'd think to myself, "I'm not going to hit that rock … I'm *not* going to hit that rock." But invariably, I'd hit the rock. Why? Because I was looking at the rock and my tire went where my eyes were focused. However, if after seeing a rock in my path I shifted my focus a few inches away from the rock, my bicycle tire went where I was focused, and I missed the rock.

This same truth is why driver's ed instructors tell us to "aim high" in the road. It keeps us aware of potential problems ahead (which we could equate to Toads), and keeps our car from moving erratically within our lane.

Bottom line, setting goals gives us a clear focus and a road map to follow. When we have such a map and we're focused on our goals, Toads are less likely to take us off course.

If you have a goal to remove Toads from your life, then here's a suggestion you can do right now: Write some goals for yourself that correspond to some of the suggestions in this "Tools for Toad Killers" section. Be sure to go over each one to make sure they're S.M.A.R.T. If your goals are large, break them down into more bite-sized chunks, and make sure those smaller goals are S.M.A.R.T., too. Be sure to include a time-of-completion, and add them to your calendar.

BONUS: To energize your motivation for accomplishing your goals, write out at least a half-dozen benefits you'll receive as a result of accomplishing each goal. Be sure to write them out, don't just think about them. If you don't like writing by hand, type them and then print them out.

The final challenge is to post those benefits alongside your goals someplace you'll see them every day. Shorter, clearly articulated goals with an accompanying list of benefits for achieving those goals will greatly enhance your likelihood of accomplishing them. Which, as you are now aware, will help keep Toads out of your life!

Do not worry about tomorrow, for tomorrow will worry about itself.
Each day has enough trouble of its own.
- *Jesus (Matthew 6:34)*

Chapter 23

Relieve Stress

S tress is a part of every person's life. In fact, our bodies actually need a certain amount of stress in order to function optimally. That said, *too much* stress is not healthy. Excessive stress is found in schools, the home, and the workplace, and it has many causes, such as disconnected relationships, disorganization, or too much to do (which can be caused by a Toad that won't let you say, "No"). Left unchecked, too much stress causes a ripple effect of problems, and it is, by nature, a breeding ground for Toads.

Over the years, I've come to realize that "stress" is simply a socially acceptable way to say, "I don't feel like I'm in control." Think about it. If my computer isn't doing what it's supposed to do, then I'm not really in control anymore ... but I tell people I'm stressed because my computer isn't working right. When my workday is getting away from me and things aren't going the way I want, I'm no longer feeling in control, but I tell people I'm stressed. When deadlines get changed and projects are coming due faster than my schedule will allow, I no longer feel in control, but I tell people I'm stressed.

This truth applies just about everywhere. If you need something for the home and you spend the day traveling from store to store but nobody has what you need, what you want to happen (finding the right gizmo) is not happening, and you start feeling like you're losing control. But, when someone asks how you're doing, you say that you're stressed because you can't find what you need.

Nobody wants to say they're starting to feel out of control, because any such statement would be perceived as admitting we are somehow weak or incapable. In polite society, the word "stressed" still means we're losing control, but instead of leading to critiques about being weak, being stressed becomes a cue for people to offer empathy. And, sometimes it's a cue for others to refrain from adding more to our plate.

Now, after saying all that, for the remainder of this chapter I'll predominately use the word *stress*, mainly because it's the word that everybody understands. But hang on to what I just explained, because it's going to help you eliminate Toads.

Taking a Stress Inventory

Since Toads love stressful environments (stress and fear often go hand-in-hand), we can take a lesson from battlefield commanders and survey the "stress" battlefield. From there you can develop strategies for removing or minimizing stress, and, as a natural ripple-effect, starve out some Toads.

To do this, first take an inventory on how you *relieve* stress. People do this in many ways, but know that some methods are much healthier than others. If you find that your stress-relief methods include watching a lot of television, over-eating, or escaping through drugs or alcohol, know that these activities often produce a bumper crop of additional Toads which—guess what—cause more stress! Those are unhealthy stress-relief methods that end up taking away from your well-being, not adding to it.

What follows is a list of ideas offered by many health care professionals as healthy ways to alleviate stress. If stress is a problem for you and you're not doing much on the following list, you might look for ways to incorporate some of these activities into your life.

Listening to or Playing Music. This has been used for centuries as a method for reducing stress, but it's been only recently that research has told us why it works. Without going into all the scientific reasons, suffice it to say that either playing or listening to music will help – a lot. But, so you know, Rap will probably not do the trick. Mozart and soft piano are highly recommended.

Talking with a Good Friend. Good friends are those who can listen well. The term I like to use when someone "needs to talk" is *zero criticism*. No advice. No shoulds. No oughts. If you have someone who can do this for you, you are a very lucky person indeed (review Chapter 18 for more info on Establishing Friendships).

Eating Healthy. Many people (myself included) find the refrigerator to be a great friend when stress comes down hard and no one else is around. But "stress eating" is not healthy, and neither are trips to fast food restaurants. By regularly eating high-fiber foods with plenty of fruits and veggies, we keep our blood sugar more even and stress loses some of its footing.

Laughing. When they say laugher is the best medicine, they're not too far off the mark. Laugher increases our intake of oxygen and stimulates our heart and lungs, with the ripple-effect being better blood flow. Some medical professionals have found that even a minute of hearty laughter can produce the same heart-rate as 10 minutes on a rowing machine.

Drinking Tea. Teas have many medicinal effects on us, all without the intense caffeine buzz produced by drinking coffee. For example, Green Tea has a natural amino-acid that produces a calming effect, as does Black Tea. Many tea drinkers will attest to how much calmer they feel after indulging in a cup of warm, aromatic tea.

Praying / Meditating. Numerous studies have revealed that prayer and meditation have excellent health benefits, including lower stress levels. I've heard it said that *Prayer* is talking to God, whereas

Meditation is listening to God. Whenever you center your thoughts in an atmosphere of peace, you're going to get benefits. As a spiritual person, I regularly practice what I read in 1 Peter 5:7, which says "Cast all your anxiety on him, because he cares for you."

Walking, or Other Exercise. Without a doubt, exercise has been researched until the cows came home, and there's definitely a direct correlation between exercise and stress-relief. In some research, it's been shown that exercise can actually reverse damage to the brain caused by stressful events. Enough said. Go for a walk!

Getting Good Sleep. Too many people shortchange themselves on sleep, thinking they can "get by." However, at the Center for Workplace Excellence, I've done studies with clients and they were amazed at how much calmer they were with the proper amount of sleep for their body. There are certain chemical reactions that occur only when you sleep, so if you're not sleeping enough, you're setting yourself up to experience unneeded stress.

Deep Breathing. Go ahead, try it. You know you want to. Right now, while you're reading this book, take in a very deep breath using your abdomen, not your shoulders. Your shoulders shouldn't move at all – just take in as much air as you can while extending your belly. Do that a few times and you can feel immediate effects. This is probably the most convenient way to drop your stress levels in very short order.

Now that you know ways to alleviate stress, it's also a good idea to inventory what stresses you, and why. According to Ellen Carni, Ph.D., writing in the legal journal *Forum*, a healthy approach to inventorying your stress is to write down all your routine tasks and your personal attitudes toward them. This doesn't have to be an ongoing activity, just do it over the course of a day or two. The simple exercise of writing out your thoughts helps you identify your mental framework. Like in the story *A Matter of Focus* (chapter 16), writing can focus you on what you're doing right – and help free you from Criticism Toads!

While you're at it, you can also journal about past situations in which you found yourself stressed, and also times when you were successful at overcoming major obstacles. By mentally reviewing each situation as you make journal entries about them, you reinforce your achievement mindset, which gives you added integrity and reinforces winning strategies for upcoming pressure situations.

By realizing what works for you in reducing your own unique stressors, you can develop strategies for countering those events that still seem to get your blood pressure up and your muscles tense.

Eating Frogs

When *Living Toad Free* was first published in 2003, I received a phone call from Brian Tracy's office. Brian Tracy had just come out with a book entitled *Eat That Frog*. They wanted me to cease and desist selling our book, claiming copyright infringement. I laughed, and explained to the person on the phone that Toad Killing and Eating Frogs were two totally different metaphors.

Eat That Frog is about time management. It's about prioritizing your workday, and putting the most difficult thing first on your list, so you don't procrastinate on it all day long. The concept comes from the saying, "Eat a live frog for breakfast and nothing worse can happen to you all day." It so happens that I first saw that saying on a T-shirt in Winslow, AZ back in 1984, and bought that shirt for my dad, who wore it for years.

Toad Killing, which you now know is about removing obstacles to success, has a much broader scope than Eating Frogs (prioritizing and time management). That said, I believe that a great way to reduce stress is to "Eat That Frog" and get the most difficult thing off your plate first thing in the morning, because then you won't have the associated stress hanging over your head all day long.

In fact, procrastinating in any capacity adds stress. Unfortunately, some people are naturally wired to put off making decisions (Example, Myers-Briggs Type Indicator, strong Perceiver score, and DISC profile low D score). Just realize that the longer you put things off, the more your task list begins to fill your mind (much like a Toad does), and the more it overcrowds your mental circuits as time goes on. If you have a natural proclivity to put things off, one of the best things you can do is find a close friend who stays on top of things, and ask him or her to help you prioritize and set deadlines (see *Setting Goals*, chapter 22).

Givers have to set limits because takers rarely do.
- Irma Kurtz

Chapter 24

Set Healthy Boundaries

Boundaries are put in place so we know who is responsible for what. We find them in suburban neighborhoods in the form of fences, in the military in the form of paygrades and operational units, and in the workplace in the form of departments and teams. Boundaries that are well-established keep lines of responsibility clear, whereas boundaries that are missing or falling apart do not. And when boundaries are falling apart, Toads often find their way in. In fact, when boundaries are falling apart, most of the time there's a Toad somewhere orchestrating the collapse.

In relationships, boundaries are the rules and cutoff points we put in place to protect ourselves. Think about the yellow lines in the middle of a road. These "boundaries" are for everyone's protection to keep drivers aware of where they should and should not be. Similarly, relationship boundaries can protect us from being "stepped-on," or prevent us from bowling over others with an overbearing attitude.

Christopher Avery, writing in *Training and Development*, says that one of the keys to effective teams in the workplace is setting and maintaining healthy boundaries. The following scenario is offered by Avery:

A team leader walks into a meeting eight minutes late. Everyone else was there on time. When the leader asked if everyone was

101

ready to start, Ned, one of the team members, said, "No." Ned then confronted the team leader. "We all agreed to start and end team meetings on time. Everyone else was ready to start this meeting on the hour. Do we need a different agreement with you about this?"

This scenario definitely shows Ned maintaining a boundary, but I do want to point out that healthy boundaries work best when mutual respect exists. Done with a productive and respectful tone of voice, the above scenario works. But if Ned's voice tone was demeaning and dripping with sarcasm, that team's foundation could easily become seriously cracked.

But let's also consider the alternative. Suppose the team leader showed up late and nobody said anything? What if they just remained quiet and let resentment fester in their hearts? Or what if they just decided to become passive-aggressive? Getting upset but not doing or saying anything about it creates Toad fodder.

In the illustration above, Ned was working to maintain healthy boundaries (assuming his voice tone was respectful). But, sometimes people get angry when boundaries are crossed, and that can be bad.

Dealing with Anger

Every upsetting situation is an opportunity to learn and grow. When people become angry, it's usually due to one of two reasons:

1. Something is happening they don't want to have happen.
2. Something is not happening that they want to have happen.

And let's take our understanding of anger even further. I learned a long time ago from my mentor that whenever people get upset, they're almost always upset with themselves at a fundamental level.

Chew on that one, if you will. It took me a long time to come to grips with that. But, I've come to see that he was right. I found that when I get angry, it's almost always an opportunity for me to grow and become more mature (some might say more responsible).

With that in mind, check your own heart. Whenever you become upset, what is it that you did or didn't do that contributed to your frustration or anger? What could have you done differently to prevent whatever happened from happening? And if it's the other way around, what could you have done to be a catalyst to bring about whatever you wanted to have happen, that didn't happen?

Usually you can find something to adjust within yourself. As my mentor put it, this is part of taking responsibility and setting new boundaries for myself. Using Toad lingo, I might say, "I can identify the Toad within myself, and either get rid of it or get around it."

If you find you are upset at someone else's behavior toward you, it may be that you simply have not set a clear boundary. The solution? Study up on boundaries and get some in place! Having courage to draw boundaries is a valuable ability that makes any home or workplace more effective.

Signs you may have weak or nonexistent boundaries:

You are socially anxious / worried that people don't like you.
You're worried that people talk about you behind your back.
You seek approval from other people / try to impress others.
You believe others are using you for their own gain.
You regularly bicker about anything with anyone.
You have either really awesome relationships, or really bad ones.
You feel you have to save everyone and/or fix their problems.
You pre-empt what you say or do with plausible excuses.
You make just about every conversation about you.
You say what you think people want to hear.
You work to control the emotions of others.
You have a difficult time saying "no" to others.

This list is *not* exhaustive, and many other issues can arise when people do not have healthy boundaries. But look again at the list. Can you just imagine how many different Toads can be causing those things? And can you imagine how much better life could be for anyone who can eliminate the Toads causing these problems?

103

If any of the statements on the previous page describe you, then I highly recommend the book *Boundaries* by Dr. Henry Cloud and Dr. John Townsend. It offers an abundance of examples and helpful tips for establishing healthy boundaries in relationships, and I guarantee you will be removing obstacles to success if you replace any of those behaviors with healthy boundaries.

That said, if you are unfamiliar with setting boundaries, be aware that some of the material in *Boundaries* will cause you to think long and hard, and you may need time to heal from past wounds as you work through the book. But do know that there's a lot of excellent content in that book, and it needs to be truly digested over time, not just gulped down in a weekend of reading.

By the way, if you're a person who has a difficult time saying "no" and you are always accommodating other people's needs, you are probably being harassed by Guilt Toads, and maybe a few more. In addition to *Boundaries* by Cloud and Townsend, allow me also to recommend *When I Say No, I Feel Guilty* by Manuel J. Smith. Either or both books will offer help for setting healthy boundaries in those situations.

Common sense is not so common.
- Voltaire

Chapter 25

Be Intelligent

What does it mean to be intelligent? Forget standard IQ tests; they only measure memorization and retention, the capacity for language and math puzzles, and the ability to take tests. People with high IQ's have done a lot of stupid things.

Tina Christopherson had one of the highest IQ's on record. Her IQ was a staggering 189. Nonetheless, she nourished one of her Toads into a monster, and it made her stupid. Here's what happened:

Tina was terrified that she would die of stomach cancer like her mother. To ward off this fate, she went on long fasts during which she ate nothing and drank great quantities of water. Sometimes she drank as much as four gallons a day. On February 17, 1977, Tina finally pushed her kidneys into failure at her home in Florida. Water migrated into her lungs, and she drowned on dry land at the age of 29.

The poor woman, even with an exceptional IQ, allowed a Toad to grow inside her mind to the point that it destroyed her.

Whereas IQ measures one form of intelligence, Harvard psychologist Howard Gardner takes a different view. He says intelligence is the capacity to solve [real world] problems and fashion products.

According to Gardner's perspective, Tina Christopherson lacked true intelligence. Despite her phenomenal IQ, she was unable to muster her brainpower to solve her problems or fashion the products her brilliant mind was capable of constructing.

As we have seen throughout this book, Toads prevent the accomplishing of goals, the solving of problems, and the fashioning of products. Toads can make people do stupid things, no matter how much brain power God has provided them.

That's a bold statement I just made, so let's consider it. If intelligence is the capacity to solve problems and fashion products, how can we define stupidity? At the risk of oversimplification, we can sum it up with an old Chinese proverb:

When a finger points at the moon, the imbecile looks at the finger.

In other words, stupidity is a failure to perceive the significant. But guess what? People can do stupid things (by not perceiving the significant) when, in fact, they are actually quite intelligent. The reason? Toads can get in the way of clear thinking. Often it is not a lack of brain power, but the presence of Toads preventing us from realizing what is relevant in our situations and our relationships.

I know several people who are thought to be stupid by others because they are not perceiving relevant factors in a relationship or a situation. But I also know those people are NOT stupid. I've been killing Toads for a long time, and I can see Toads at work in their lives, holding them back and preventing their growth.

But let's keep going. For another perspective on intelligence, let's consider what J. Martin Klotsche, former Chancellor of the University of Wisconsin at Milwaukee, once stated:

Intelligence is derived from two words --- *inter* and *legere* --- *inter* meaning "between," and *legere* meaning "to choose." An intelligent person, therefore, is one who has learned "to choose between."

This brings us to the question of, "How can we be intelligent?" I believe both Gardner's and Klotsche's perspectives have substance (although I would add *choose wisely* to Klotsche's definition). So, by combining both Klotsche's and Gardner's perspectives, we get the following:

If we are to be intelligent, we must have:

1) A capacity to solve problems and fashion products, and
2) The ability to choose wisely between (or among) our options.

Can you do those things? I'm confident you can, so therefore you have intelligence. But as we strive to remove obstacles in the way of our success, we must regularly be on the lookout for Toads that prevent us from solving problems, fashioning products, and choosing wisely.

Toads that commonly get in the way of our intelligence are Fear Toads (whatever the fear might be) as well as Lack-of-Information-so-Therefore-I-Can't-Decide Toads. These types of Toads are often eliminated simply by seeking out additional pertinent information with which to make a decision. Just keep in mind that as you seek out more information, you might find you have a Fear of Failure or a Fear of Criticism Toad.

Other Toads that get in the way of our intelligence are Delusion Toads, Complacency Toads, and the ever-passively malevolent Go-Along-to-Get-Along Toads.

As Toad Killers, we increase our intelligence by making wise choices. Yes, we will make mistakes along the way (see the next chapter about making mistakes), but if we are intelligent, we learn as we go. Even if we learn slowly, we're still increasing our ability to solve problems, fashion products, and make wiser decisions. And, in so doing, we'll be eliminating many nasty, success-inhibiting Toads along the way.

The man who makes no mistakes does not usually make anything.
- *Theodore Roosevelt*

Chapter 26

Make Only New Mistakes

Everyone makes mistakes. *Everyone.* But did you know that mistakes are simply opportunities for learning? Making old mistakes (that is, making the same mistakes over and over) forms cesspools, and those become breeding grounds for Toads. Therefore, a key to your success is to make only new mistakes.

Every time you fail or make a mistake (and in case you haven't thought about it, you'll be doing that the rest of your life), learn from that mistake and establish a new standard or boundary.

Allow me to share a little phrase to remember whenever you make a mistake or something doesn't go well. Essentially, you "look three places":

Look up, Look down, and Look ahead

To *look up* means to identify what went well. To *look down* means to identify what didn't go so well. And to *look ahead* means to figure out how something could be done differently in the future.

By looking in these three places when you make a mistake, you have a tool that reduces the likelihood of making the same mistake a second time, and that minimizes the chances of any Toads gaining a foothold. If you keep making the same mistakes, Guilt Toads and Victim Toads can rear their ugly heads as they move to slow you down – or stop you altogether.

109

By the way, sometimes mistakes can result in wonderful things. For example, consider the following:

The first chocolate chip cookies were a mistake. The chunks of chocolate were supposed to melt and cause the entire batch of dough to become chocolate dough. It didn't work, but now have cool cookies.

John and Keith Kellogg accidently left a pot of boiled grain on the stove for way too long. By accident, they invented Corn Flakes.

Spencer Silver was trying to make a super strong adhesive at 3M, but it wasn't working. The glue kept coming off things—and easily. For 10 years Silver tried telling people his "mistake" still had value, but no one listened. Then, 10 years later, someone finally saw a value, and Post-It Notes were invented.

William Greatbatch was working on a device to record heart rhythms, but accidently used a wrong resistor when assembling one. The result was not a recording device, but a device that could send regular electrical signals to the heart. When implanted in the human body, Greatbatch's *pacemaker* would keep hearts beating steadily.

And so, sometimes very good things can result from mistakes, but overall that's pretty rare. Therefore, remember that a failed attempt does not define the person who made the mistake. When we make mistakes, our main job is to *learn from them*. Recall the story about Thomas Edison, who was asked how he felt after failing more than 10,000 times to make a working light bulb. Edison's response was classic. He said that he did not fail 10,000 times, but that he merely found 10,000 ways that would not work.

In other words, he learned what NOT to do each time it didn't work. And, while I doubt he used my phrase, Edison was well-practiced in the philosophy of Look up, Look down, and Look ahead.

The bottom line: You will remove many obstacles on your road to success by following the advice of a wise old grandmother:

Make Only New Mistakes – Not Old Ones

(That is, unless you're making chocolate chip cookies.)

Section 6:
Final Thoughts

*'The Room of 1000 Toads' is an adaptation of 'The Room of 1000 Demons,' from the book *Do One Thing Different* by Bill O'Hanlon. It has been rewritten to fit the Toad concept with permission.

Chapter 27

The Room of 1000 Toads*

Sammy centipede was nervous. By special invitation he was attending a gathering of centipedes that hoped to gain enlightenment. He was standing rank and file with all the other centipedes, dressed in their ceremonial white socks and white tennis shoes. The centipede leaders lined up before the students, and then the high priest centipede flowed out of his cave. The whole scene, already silent, became focused as all eyes and ears turned to the high priest.

"This is the ceremony of the Room of 1000 Toads," the high priest announced. "It is the ceremony to achieve enlightenment, and it occurs only once every 100 years. If you choose not to go through it now, you will have to wait another 100 years. To help you make this decision we will tell you what the ceremony involves.

"In order to enter the Room of 1000 Toads, you simply open the door and walk in. The Room of 1000 Toads is not very big. Once you enter, the door will close behind you. There is no doorknob on the inside of the door. To get out, you will have to walk all the way through the room, find the door on the other side, open the door – which is unlocked – and come out. Then you will be enlightened.

"The room is called the Room of 1000 Toads because there are 1000 Toads inside. You should know that these Toads have the ability to take on the form of your worst fears. As soon as you enter the room, the Toads will take on the appearance of everything that frightens you and holds you back. If you have a fear of heights, a Toad will get under you and appear as a narrow ledge on a tall building. If you have a fear of spiders, the Toads will transform themselves into terrifying eight-legged creatures. Whatever your fears, the Toads will take on the appearance of those images in your mind and make them seem real. In fact, they'll be so compellingly real that it will be very difficult to remember that they're not.

"No one can come in and rescue you. This is part of the rules of the ceremony. If you choose to enter the Room of 1000 Toads, you must leave it on your own.

"You should know that some centipedes never come out. They go into the Room of 1000 Toads and become paralyzed with fright. They stay stuck in their fears until they die.

"If you do not want to take the risk of entering the Room of 1000 Toads, that is fine. You do not have to enter the room. You can wait and come back in another 100 years and try again. But my advice to you is this: If you're not ready, get ready.

"If you want to enter the room, we have two suggestions that will help you. The first is this: When you enter the Room of 1000 Toads, remember that what they show you is not real. It's all just imagery taken from your own mind. Do not buy into it. It is an illusion. But keep in mind that every centipede that went in the room before you knew that. This is a very difficult thing to remember.

"The second suggestion has been more helpful for those centipedes who have made it out the exit door: Once you enter the room, no matter what you see, no matter what you think, no matter what you hear, keep your feet moving. If you keep your feet moving, you will eventually get to the other side, find the door, and come out. Then you will be enlightened."

I set before you life or death, blessing or curse. Therefore, choose life.
- *Deuteronomy 30:19*

Chapter 28

Final Thoughts

The bottom line principle in the previous chapter, *The Room of 1000 Toads*, and in fact to all of life, is *keep your feet moving*. In other words, keep doing something! As I mentioned earlier in the book, everyone has motivation, but some people experience resistance and then stop moving. As we learned from Coach Hatfield, "It's no sin to be blocked, only to stay blocked."

Successful people work to gain experience, establish true friendships, and stay aware of what's going on around them. They also listen to learn their true vocation, they set goals, and they take responsibility for their actions. To stay heathy, they set appropriate boundaries, and when things get tough, they wisely find ways to unwind and relieve their stress. Successful people also strive to be resourceful and use their skills intelligently for the betterment of their fellow man. And, when they make mistakes, they learn from them.

Throughout life you will face obstacles. Remove them! Toads may occasionally slow you down, but now you know their tricks, and now you have tools to remove them from your path.

As I wrap up this book, you should know that sometimes people have Toads that have been around a long time. Sometimes those Toads have grown so large, they are difficult to remove, and they can't be squashed by just one foot. Therefore, if you ever discover a

115

Toad is bigger than your foot, know that it's okay to ask for help! Someone will be more than happy to help you squash it.

Secondly, you may discover certain Toads that are firmly dug in and don't want to leave. Removing such Toads may require help from "upstairs," so don't be afraid to ask for that kind of help, either.

With that, I encourage you to hang on to your faith. God didn't create us to be stymied or stopped by pesky Toads. Fear is the power behind most Toads, and I'd like you to know that when you have faith, fear is minimalized. And so, as you set out to rid your life of Toads (aka Removing Obstacles to Success), may you have tremendous victory. And feel free to contact me with your successes. I'd love to hear about them.

PS. As the late Dennis Rader and I both acknowledged, there is no way to *truly* be Toad free, for on this earth, we will always encounter obstacles that try to hold us back. But that doesn't mean we can't take out as many Toads as possible along the way. Therefore, it was always one of our fun catchphrases to say,

Whoever dies with the most dead Toads, wins.

With that in mind, happy hunting! And may you be Toad Free.

A Tribute to Dr. Dennis R. Rader

Dennis Rader was not your typical professor. If he'd been typical, I wouldn't be writing this. Dennis was the best I've ever known at using the Socratic Method to get students to think. The assignments he gave were far outside the norm, but in assigning them he got students to think way outside the box. I would like to think that Dennis's students learned more from him than from other instructors, and that the lessons they learned through him enabled them to live a much more fulfilling life.

This was certainly true for me.

I first met Dennis when he was an adjunct professor for Southern Illinois University's extension program in San Diego, where he taught Educational Psychology in my undergraduate program. He asked great open-ended questions and encouraged students to debate and defend their perspectives about the human condition and how we learn.

My life was forever changed the day Dennis gave us an assignment almost as an afterthought as we were getting ready to leave class. "Oh by the way," he said, "in my book *Hogs on Ice* you'll find a chapter titled 'Teachers as Toad Killers.' Read that chapter and write a one-page paper entitled, 'Myself as a Toad Killer.'" I'm sure we all looked at him with expressions that communicated, "What on earth are you talking about?" because he just smiled and said, "Read the chapter and you'll know what I'm talking about."

I had already been running my own company as a management coach for several years, working one-on-one with managers at multiple levels within organizations to identify obstacles that were holding them back and then finding ways around them. With that background, the concept in "Teachers as Toad Killers" immediately resonated with me. In that chapter, Dennis told a story about Coach Hatfield, a basketball coach who used the metaphor of a Toad to represent obstacles that dwell within our minds and keep us from achieving our true potential. I couldn't believe the power of Dennis's story. It was an amazingly simple metaphor to help people wrap their minds around the idea of "old tapes" or fears that hold us back. I couldn't stop telling people what I called, "The Toad Story."

At our very next class, I waited until an opportune sidebar moment and said, "Dr. Rader, you know that Toad story? It is extremely powerful. It needs to be more than just a chapter in your book – it needs to be a book all by itself." Dennis's next words changed my life. He said, "Would you like to write it with me?"

We worked on the project sporadically, and when Dennis moved to Mississippi and then Kentucky we lost track of each other because he didn't believe in email. Thankfully, Dennis eventually warmed up to technology and we reconnected. I finally flew to Kentucky in 2003 where we sequestered ourselves in a hotel for several days to finish writing *Living Toad Free*.

Dennis was not only a phenomenal teacher, the synergistic ideas that filled the room when the two of us got together were unbelievable. I can't tell you how many times we'd sit down to talk and then kick ourselves an hour later for not turning on a tape recorder.

After *Living Toad Free* was published, Dennis would occasionally accompany me to conduct training for my clients. Whenever possible, we would also visit bookstores and do book signings together.

We kept in touch throughout the years, getting together from time to time and always talking about doing a second edition of Toads. Unfortunately, other projects always seemed to take the front burner, and now I'm re-working the book by myself. In February of 2013, Dennis passed away from a heart attack.

Dennis once told me that, "Writing is the highest form of teaching, because your writing impacts people you will never meet, and it also stays around long after you're gone."

True words. Dennis and I regularly called each other to share whenever we heard how the Toad story impacted people's lives. There was the 40-year-old woman we heard from who, after reading *Living Toad Free*, decided to go back to college and finish her degree. That gave her some needed credentials, and now she is the executive director for a large non-profit organization.

Another story was about a middle-aged man who, after participating in a discussion group about getting rid of Toads, decided not to leave his wife. We heard dozens of such stories. We even heard from a woman in Pennsylvania whose life was so changed by the Toad story that she asked for (and received) permission to conduct *Living Toad Free* workshops for the staff of the large university where she worked.

Dennis, wherever you are now, I hope you are even more aware that your Coach Hatfield story not only changed my life, but it also changed the lives of thousands of people you never had the opportunity to meet—and that it will continue to do so now that you're gone. You are missed. Rest in peace.

- Dan Bobinski

Acknowledgements

This book is the result of decades of study and work. In reality, the list of people who contributed to the content—and deserve thanks—could fill the book. But, I'm limiting myself to a page.

First and foremost I must thank my awesome wife, Jeralynne. She is, by far, my favorite editor and also my favorite person in the world. She supports me 100% in all that I do. Thank you, love!!!

I must also acknowledge the people whose stories populate this book—both the ones who said I could mention them, and the ones who preferred to stay anonymous. Thank you! I must also thank Alex Goodman, because Alex, you started this way back when you taught me how to be a Toad Killer before either of us knew what one was. Thanks also to Robert Croker, Judy Paxton, Jonathan Neuneker, Ana Hollinger, Noriko Tsuchiya, and James Bono, too. I'm also indebted to Rose Sulfridge, who provides more support than she knows, and also to my dad, Eugene Bobinski, who showed me what it meant to have integrity. Of course, I must also thank my daughter Abbey, who captures my heart every day, and gives me unbelievable joy, and also my faithful pup Shadow, who, though no longer a puppy, consistently reminds us all of the importance of family time. Lastly, and most importantly, I thank my Lord and Savior for His amazing love. I certainly hope He doesn't mind our twisted humor when we say things like, "Whoever dies with the most dead Toads, wins." But it's my guess that God has a sense of humor, so I think we're okay.

Happy Toad hunting, everyone! May you all live Toad Free!